BAD WITH MONEY

CRITICAL MONEY SKILLS YOU NEED TO SURVIVE - AND NOBODY TAUGHT YOU.

ASHISH TEWARI

Made with ♥ on the Notion Press Platform
www.notionpress.com

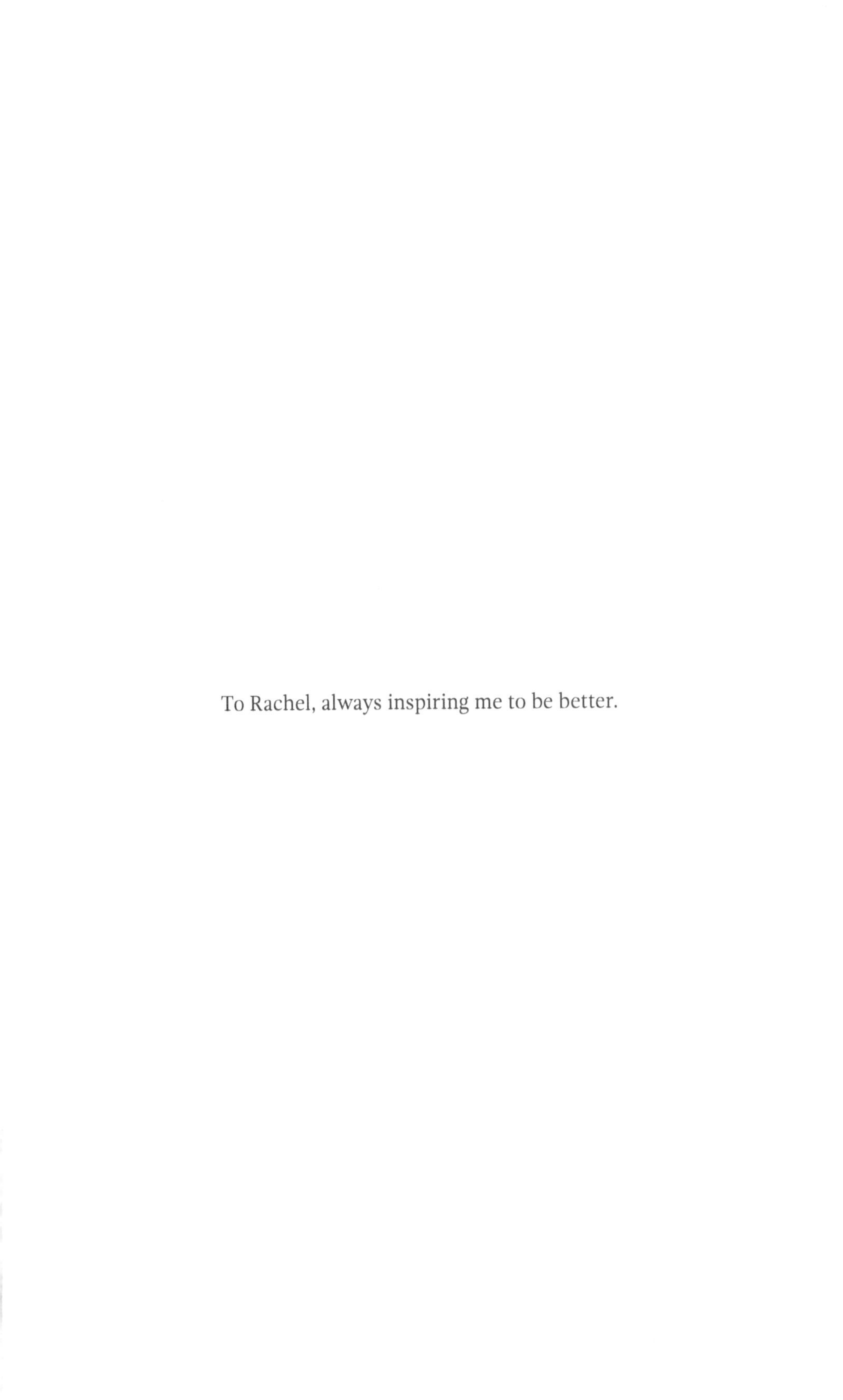

To Rachel, always inspiring me to be better.

Contents

Contents

Contents

Foreword

Your Money And Your Life

This book isn't financial advice. I'm not a financial advisor, wealth manager, stock market guru, agent, or broker.

It isn't a career guide, a life lesson, self-help, spiritual upliftment, or the like.

It isn't some super-detailed encyclopedia of each & every financial terms, products and concepts.

So, what *is* it?

The last few decades, I've often seen the same money-related thoughts come up regularly.

- *Why did I do that?*
- *I wish I'd known, back then.*
- *This is too confusing.*
- *Someone should've taught me this better.*

There are times when you realize you've made a huge money mistake, and try to figure out how and why... so you don't repeat it.

I see how those mistakes impact not only me, but others around me.

I see so many more people struggling with the same issues.

Now, I've made a *lot* of mistakes with money. I've been an idiot, often making unplanned, random choices, then struggling to handle the outcome.

And I'd always assumed, this is how life is, for most of us. The future would just be the same.

I would think - **I'm bad with money.**

One's own bad decisions and mistakes... can be a hard thing to think about.

All the more so with money - there's so much emotional, social value we attach to money. It represents, in our head, our intelligence, our reliability and responsibility, our maturity, our social status. Our hopes and dreams.

And when we fail, it feels uncomfortable, painful, and embarrassing. Shameful.

It makes one defensive. Angry, guilty, frustrated... and the only thing one wants, in that moment, is to push away those thoughts, drown them out.

Sometimes, we try to forget those thoughts by replacing them with alcohol, Netflix, infinitely-scrolling Insta, the news.

We attack the person who brought it up, who made you think. Argue and fight.

We point fingers. Blame the economy, our job, our boss, regulations, family, immigrants, our visa status, reservations, nepotism, office politics, biases, gender, education, personality, language, skin color, height, weight, dressing, whatever, *anything but ourselves.*

We shut everything out and work harder, and harder, and harder... till we drop dead of a heart attack.

And this is easy, comforting even. If the fault lies in things outside our control, we can't be responsible. Suffering under an unfair system gives us a sense of righteous martyrdom, but also frees us from the much greater effort and initiative of doing something about it.

Then, if we do decide to do something, we choose the wrong things.

We fixate on a guide. A guru, a finfluencer, a CA, some random uncle in our society, a TV or YT channel - someone who can tell us what to do, and we can blindly follow them, free of taking responsibility for our own choices.

(*We daydream*) on that next great thing that will solve all problems... if it happens. The next raise, promotion, job shift. The next big deal, order, contract. The lottery. Finding some long-lost rich chacha. Saving a billionaire's only child from a speeding truck.

Or, we procrastinate, because figuring out what to do is hard. Our situation is unique to us, so there are no easy precedents or guidelines that work exactly for us.

We swear to figure it out, and fix it, starting... tomorrow. Next month, when salary comes. Next New Year's Day resolutions. Next...

And life would go on, as usual.

But somewhere along the way, I had a realization, a life-changing epiphany.

Thinking about your own mistakes is hard to digest, because you only have half the idea.

- **I was bad with money.**

There's second half, that makes all the difference.

- **How do I not be bad with money?**

Yes, so you made poor choices, for a thousand good reasons... **but they don't matter anymore.**

It doesn't feel good, it's time for something better.

Starting today, you stop being bad with money.

That's **what this book is.**

When I've looked at my mistakes, I'd say, *"I wish I knew (that) before."*

Well, here's all the things I wish I knew before. It's taken a while to collect, from books, courses, videos, blogs, workshops, podcasts, consultations, and people, but mostly, from bitter experience - but every one is a solution to a mistake made, so I don't repeat it.

All of it, it's what I wish I'd known, *before* I started handling personal finance.

And here *you* are, starting to handle personal finance!

Now, you may have different situations, different money problems, of your own.

But we've both made (*or are about to make*) many of the same mistakes - and hopefully, by the time you finish reading, I've helped you avoid, or at least mitigate, some of them.

• • •

Preface

How to read this book

You *could* finish this book in a few days, and hopefully you'll still find it entertaining & useful... but I have another suggestion.

Go slow.

Read a chapter a week - then try stuff out. It's not just by reading, but by doing, that you're going to learn and internalize what this is all about - and you can't do it in a week.

The reason you're here, on this page, and hopefully the rest that follow, is because you want to make your life better. **That doesn't happen fast.** Trying to do it fast will have the opposite effect, rushing into hasty, emotional decisions, and leaving you with burned fingers - and an unreasonable desire to find, and throw a brick at, the author.

As you go, chapter by chapter, spend time researching concepts. Finance is complex; every person's situation and journey is different.

Read, then research. Look up terms, explanations, youtube tutorials, browse wikipedia, ask your favorite AI assistant. We're starting from a basic foundation, but to build knowledge that's relevant and useful, specifically to you, you're going to have to do a lot of the work for yourself.

There's a suggested to-do list after each chapter, but the real learning - and fun - will come as you play around, make your own modifications, test stuff out. The list isn't some exercise to be completed; each item on it, a new field to be explored.

That's the only way you'll absorb it, remember it, and *like* it.

Only *then*, you'll be able to *do* it.

And only *then*... will it work for you.

What I've done, for myself, is a custom-built process created over years... with variations relevant for my goals and priorities. It may not work for you, as is. You're going to have to start with the base, and then build your own structure on top, based on what's important for you.

So keep this in mind, and as you start reading, read when & where you have free time, access to the internet, and an open excel sheet.

Keep notes, move carefully, pay attention to the details... and things will turn out fine.

• • •

Prologue

Whispers

She's coming... go, ask her, when is she paying you back?

Why sir is still taking train? Why he's not got car? Arre at his level-

Watch, as soon as the bill comes she'll be on her phone or going to the loo. Bet laga.

I know all your friends have, we're not buying it. It's too expensive, now keep quiet...

Bhaiya, just in case, can I borrow some money for the hospital? I'm not sure if this is covered or not... no, no, I'll give it by next month, I promise...

Tell him if he wants to eat, he has to clear his tab. In full. Right now! Or get lost!

You heard, the bank sent some collection guys and they were creating one huge ruckus outside yesterday, the kids were so scared... the society chairman had to call the police!

Look at this tax return Patil... no exemptions. None! I've never seen this before...

Beta, it's ok, I don't have much expenses, don't worry, I'll be fine. Just take this, pay the school...

Just don't talk about stocks, please, ok? He gets super upset, then I have to deal with it...

How many credit cards does she even have?!

He's not dumb, he got good marks, he gets a good salary... but I don't know... we don't even spend that much...

guess he's just... just **bad with money...**

• • •

Disclaimers

And last of all before we get started, a few brief disclaimers.

1. **I'm not a certified financial advisor or wealth planner.** This book is meant to be educational by describing and explaining concepts and overviews, and suggesting approaches. It is not, and should not be taken as, formal financial advice.
2. I have mentioned multiple tools, products, companies, and categories of financial instruments. These are meant to be **examples only**, and are not be taken as endorsements for use or recommendations for investment.
3. Similarly, any references to listed companies is **not a stock buying / selling recommendation.** Popular names have been selected for familiarity and broad understanding in the Indian context; they are not endorsements.
4. Some short stories / anecdotes have been used to illustrate, via a dramatic context, situations related to and illustrative of certain financial concepts and human behaviors only. They do not represent any actual persons, companies, or situations in reality; **any resemblance to real life or any persons living or dead is coincidental, and is not intended to praise, insult, or embarass any specific persons or entities.**
5. Products and concepts in the financial and technological space evolve rapidly, and **may be outdated / obsolete at the time you read this book.** References to specific products should be taken in context of the flow, and be objectively evaluated against the latest equivalent available at the time of reading.
6. **You are expected to make all your financial decisions yourself, based on your own independent, data-driven research.**

• • •

Who's This For?

If you're in the first couple of years of your working life, this is for you.

This book is meant for anyone who wants to learn managing their personal finances, as a guide to first steps.

So, if you're feeling lost with choices, struggling with the aftermath of bad decisions, trying to figure out what to do, and what to do first, and what to not do at all, give this a try.

This book's not a comprehensive guide to advanced money management, not an in-depth dive into a comprehensive set of complex financial instruments, not an investment strategy resource. There are no deep investing insights, trading tips, chart analysis, stock picking, wealth strategy, financial management, or anything else that ends with a Lamborghini in your garage.

I'm not going to give you a specific plan or checklist. You have to do that yourself after you've seen the bigger picture.

I'm just going to **build a framework**, a way to handle the basics. Create an approach through which you can get clarity, plan. Establish good money habits to become a base on which you build your future.

If you already know the basics, and are able to handle your own money without getting in debt; if you don't go running around with cash like it's burning a hole in your pocket; then put this book back on the shelf, and walk away. It's not going to add too much to your life.

But if you do feel like you're constantly making bad money decisions - then go on reading.

We make bad money decisions all the time. Not because we want to - we may not know better, or listen to the wrong sources and get exploited, or blindly follow well-meaning, but outdated and irrelevant, advice.

It's not easy - there's a lot of information out there, and it's hard to know how, and where, to begin.

So now, let's explore some of those wealth-wasting mistakes you and I are making (*or going to!*), **and fix them.**

Let's make a structure of how to think about personal finance, so we can figure out what we want, where we are, and what we need to do.

Your money's like your dog. It doesn't have to be messy, unmanageable, or dangerous - but it *is* a responsibility. Trained right, and it can be your best friend.

If not, you get bitten.

• • •

What Makes This Book Different?

A lot of the financial literacy books I read - and the courses and workshops as well - suffered from two common complaints.

Both were very off-putting - often, they'd be the reason I would throw aside the book, or pause the course, because fundamentally, I felt something was going wrong, something I just couldn't identify with.

Before we get to those, tell me if this sounds familiar - that classic example - the *'there are two types of people' wala.*

1. Aaryyan **blows all his money** on luxuries, impressing friends, attracting women, indulging in every whim of whatever makes him happy. His ability to spend is what defines his identity. When his money runs out, he switches to credit cards, begs from family, borrows from friends, steals from customers, and finally, dies in debt and poverty, shunned by all, weeping bitter tears of regret.
   Don't be like Aaryyan.
2. Bharti is a **wise and temperate** paragon of virtue, who plans with foresight and acumen, saving large portions of her income practically from as soon as she can walk. No profligacy for her! She saves every rupee and buys only appreciating assets, blue-chip shares, reliable index funds, gold bars, landed property, FDs and her PPF. She travels by bus, and later, a sensible, reliable small car that runs for 25 years. By the time she's 50, she's settled with her own home and retirement fund.
   Do you want to be like Bharti, though?

I'd alway wonder - is it some rule, that one path will always end in disaster and sadness, and the other, always in success and happiness?

Is happiness defined, according to financial literacy, **in only making the right, 'sensible' choices?** Did Bharti not look back, and regretted a Ladakh trip avoided, a beautiful dress left in the window, a five-star meal uneaten? Did she watch Aaryyan speeding down the slippery slope of hell and not feel, even once, the smallest twinge of... envy?

Because if not, I might not have liked her much. She doesn't seem human enough.

And that's what we all are - only human. We have our desires and wants. Financial literacy shouldn't equate to asceticism - it's ok to have fun as well, provided you're not warming your present, by setting fire to your future.

Don't look at financial literacy, awareness, planning, and practice, as a purely numbers game.

What?! Heresy! No numbers in finance?! Has the author lost what little remains of his mind?

No, there will be numbers, lots of numbers, and formulae, and charts... but it isn't just numbers. If you start looking at money as a score, every rupee you spend on anything not adding to the score feels wasted. There's no room for treating yourself, and anything that's fun, gets a side of guilt slapped on.

So here's the two things that kept pissing me off, while learning about money.

One, Money is emotional, not a dry numbers exercise.

It can't be divorced from real life, and exist purely as some cerebral 'score'. Having it is good, but having it at the cost of having any kind of life, not so good. Financial literacy should be about becoming money's master, and making it work for you. Not about you working for it.

Two, Money is written about in a complicated way.

Finance tends to suffer from a kind of knowledge diarrhea. It's a complex subject, sure, but that doesn't mean knowing how to be financially literate means knowing, from the start, every nuance of every product you'll ever need, from birth to death and beyond.

When you learn regular literacy, you start with the alphabet and move up to simple, three-word sentences. This is usually enough to communicate with.

Similarly, you don't need to consider yourself financially illiterate if you can't build huge, complex, scenario-planning simulation excels that factor in finance feeds, future IRR & current NPV, live stock prices, predicted bond rates, detailed company analyses, complex balance sheets, depreciating values, projections, forecasts, economic data, the great leader's tweets, and the prophecies of Nostrodamus.

Yet any book you pick up will explain exactly this - how to go from your first paycheck to your last will and testament, in 300 pages with diagrams and formulae. It's a lot.

It can be overwhelming.

And it's unnecessary.

If you're twenty, the only thing you need to know about retirement planning is that one day you'll need it, and will have to start preparing sooner than you think.

If you're sixty, I don't need to explain compound interest to you.

Money is complicated.

So, this book isn't. Let's keep it to the basics. You're starting out, so everything I talk about, will be limited to what's relevant within a five-year window.

It can be surprisingly effective. A lot of the basics will keep going for decades, and will need the inclusion of not that many new concepts and products as you grow older; but those basics need to be absorbed well.

There can be beauty - and efficiency - in simplicity.

• • •

Starting Out

Every journey of a thousand miles begins with a single step

Ancient Chinese Proverb

CHAPTER I

Basic Concepts

Before we go ahead, there's a couple of simple, but very critical, core concepts you'll need to know and understand. These are going to be the backbone of what comes next, because they're at the heart of everything personal finance is all about.

These are the triggers of your personal finance apocalypse.

Ignoring Inflation.

Forgetting about Compounding.

Miscalculating Risk & Reward.

Giving in to Fear or Greed.

Refusing to Diversify.

Living paycheck-to-paycheck

Taxation.

• • •

CHAPTER II

Inflation

Price go up.

What costs X today, will cost X+Y tomorrow, X+Y+Z the year after, and so on. It's the way our money system is built, the way our economy runs, which ensures that everything, on average, always keeps getting more expensive.

Why that happens, has a complex historical / economic answer - out of scope for today. But it does happen, which means... we need to prepare for it.

This means the money we have today will not be the same value tomorrow - it will be less. If you got through a month with Rs. 100 today, you will need Rs. 110 next year. If you plan to buy something in 5 years (*or later*) and it costs Rs. 1 cr now, you'll need much more when the time comes to buy it. **The longer the waiting time, the higher the cost.**

So anything you were planning to buy, don't take today's cost as the baseline.

Think in terms of inflation's impact on big spends in the far future, that you know will be needed - a nice holiday, higher education (for yourself or your kids), buying a house, hospitalization, having a baby and raising a child, weddings, and most critically, retirement.

Money shrinks.

This also means - if you have Rs. 100 saved today, then even without you spending, or doing anything with it, it will be worth less tomorrow - i.e. you'll be able to buy less things with it. With enough time, all of today's savings will go to near-zero in the future - even if you didn't waste them, lose them, or mismanage them. Just doing nothing at all is enough.

Inflation Rate: the % at which stuff gets more expensive, on average. This'll always be higher than zero, as long as the country's economy is growing. Some things get more expensive faster than others, like fuel, school fees, medical costs, rent. Others are slower but still there - food, travel, utilities. It all adds up.

Assuming the inflation rate's 10% -

Inflation		
Decreasing value of today's money		
Starting	₹	1,000
Inflation Rate		10%
Year 1	₹	1,000
Year 2	₹	900
Year 3	₹	810
Year 4	₹	729
Year 5	₹	656
Year 6	₹	590
Year 7	₹	531
Year 8	₹	478
Year 9	₹	430
Year 10	₹	387

How Inflation Decreases Value

You see how, in less than ten years, you've lost over half of all you saved? Even keeping money in a bank isn't a solution - sure, you earn interest, but that's rarely higher than inflation. So, your money just loses value a little more slowly, but continuously.

• • •

Exercise -

- Find out what's the inflation rate, right now.
- Then look at the interest rate you get from your bank account.
- Subtract.
- Bank Interest % - Inflation % = Value lost of every Rs. 100, every year.

That's the rate at which you're losing money, every single minute it just sits there.

Unless... you can keep it growing faster than inflation.

That's the reason why we invest - so that every rupee you worked so hard for, and sacrificed to keep aside for a better future, can not be allowed to just... drain away.

• • •

To-Do

- Open an excel
- Lookup and enter the current inflation rate = (i1)
- Lookup the average interest you get from your bank account (nominal return) = (i2)
- (*Don't consider FDs or other investments right now, and don't consider money you'll be spending in the short term. I'm talking about the money that you're saving in the bank.*)
- Get the difference (real return) i = (i2 - i1)
- Add up the total money sitting in the bank account(s) = (P) your savings, not money meant for something else.
- I'm assuming, for simplicity, that interest and inflation are both annual, so (N) = 1 (year)
- Use this formula: $A = P*(1+(I/1))^{\wedge}N$

You know what this is?
This is the future value of today's money. *This* is how much your current money will be worth at the end of a year, by doing nothing except just sitting there.
P - A = what you lose by doing nothing.
Think about that a little.

- Change up the value of N for 2, 3, 5 years, and see what happens.

Now let's make it *real.*

- Think of a long-term goal, and calculate what you would need for that today - say, a long Europe holiday in a few years. Add up the cost of flight tickets, hotels, estimated daily spending, travel, food, activities. Reach a figure of total cost needed for that holiday.
- Do you think that *this* amount is what you will need, when you actually travel?

Nope - you'll need more.

- Use the formula you learned just now and check how much more.

- Then repeat the exercise for, say, an executive MBA from your preferred college, in 10 years.

See, how stuff starts to look more & more... unaffordable?

• • •

CHAPTER III

Compounding

"You think money grows on trees?!"
- Every exasperated parent

Compounding literally is the tree on which money grows.

Let's look at saving, now from the other side. Say, you've found someplace where you get a decent interest rate of 8%. Then your Rs. 100 saved today, will become Rs. 108 next year, and grow again by 8% the year after... and the growth is not on the original 100, but the original 100 AND the new 8 you earned, repeated for every increase.

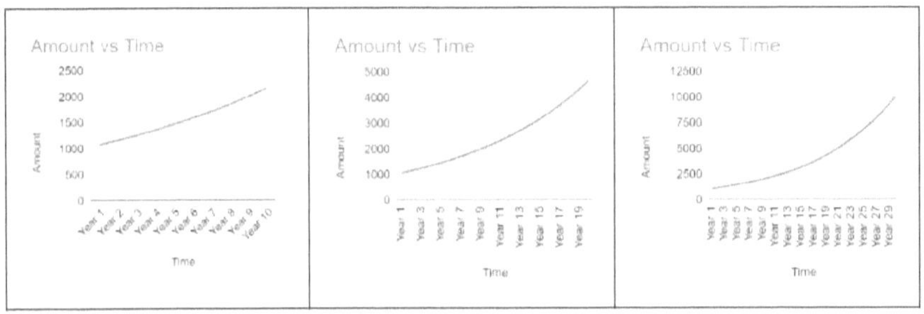

Impact of Time on Compounding

In 10 years, Rs. 1000 became 2000. *Big deal.*

In 20 years, Rs. 1000 crossed 4000. *Interesting.*

In 30 years, Rs. 1000 touched 10,000. 10X growth. *Now this is fun.*

It just takes time.

It's a *very* simple concept. Everyone gets it, immediately. And then, they forget it, because it's abstract, slow-burning, and long-term. Not a fun, exciting thing.

Why do people forget? For a short period, it looks slow and imperceptible. Dull and boring. Too small, pointless. But the longer you go, the steeper up that curve gets. And don't forget, this is all passive - it's growing on its own, with no effort from you, as long as you don't spend it.

Compounding		
Increasing value of today's money		
Starting	₹	1,000
Interest Rate %		8%
Year 1	₹	1,080
Year 2	₹	1,166
Year 3	₹	1,260
Year 4	₹	1,360
Year 5	₹	1,469
Year 6	₹	1,587
Year 7	₹	1,714
Year 8	₹	1,851
Year 9	₹	1,999
Year 10	₹	2,159

How Compounding Works

Look back at inflation. Compare those 2 tables.

If you did nothing (*i.e. saved cash money under your mattress*), then your savings will be worth less than half in ten years, because inflation would've destroyed their value.

If you had compounded, i.e. grew your money, it would have more than doubled.

These 2 forces work opposite to each other.

If your inflation rate and compounding rate are the *same*, the *number* might change, but the *value* will stay exactly the same.

What you can buy for Rs. 100 today, you'll have to buy for Rs. 236 in 10 years. Luckily, the cash you left compounding has delivered almost exactly that.

It looks like you gained, but in reality, **you've just kept pace with inflation.**

In both cases, time is the greatest factor. The longer you compound your money, without spending, the more it grows.

If you save without earning interest, you lose quickly. If you save, earning less interest than inflation, you lose slowly. But as long as you don't outpace inflation, you're inevitably losing.

It's a rigged game.

So *that's* the first goal of saving, and growing your savings. **To make sure the compounding rate (i.e. your returns) at least meets inflation.** Which also means you need to save your money (especially over the long run) in places where you get an interest or return rate that's at least meeting, or better yet, beating, inflation.

Which also means, you need to have a very clear idea of what the real inflation rate is, because that's your target. Can you beat that?

Cash in a box, won't work. A simple bank account, won't work. FDs are better... but there are yet other solutions, who offer a much bigger upside in the returns.

The downside? They differ in another important way as well - in terms of the *risk* you take.

• • •

To Do

- Open an excel
- Set P as the amount you can safely save each year.
- Put I as the simple interest you get from the bank. (Let's ignore inflation for now)
- Now make a table:

  - Col1: Year 1, Year 2, etc
  - Col2: 0 in the 1st row
  - Col3: P (this is what you are adding each year)
  - Col4: Col2 + Col3 (total available each year, adding what was there from last year)
  - Col5: Col4 * $(1+I)^1$ This is the original value + interest earned in the 1st year. Remember to keep I fixed, or just use the numeric value like 3.5% if that's what you earn in a savings bank)
  - In the 2nd row, make Col2 = 1st row Col5 value. Copy-paste the rest of Row 1.
  - Repeat for each row until you have 10 rows.

What we've done here, is a simple calculation to see how, if you can save even a small amount *consistently,* the final compounded value in 10 years, is higher than the total amount we actually put aside.

Now, we know that the real value of I is negative, because inflation is higher than simple bank account interest, so we're actually losing money over time by keeping it in the bank.

But here's where the fun part comes in. **You're not married to the bank.** There are other options to save.

- See what would have happened if you had it in an FD (changing I to 6.6%), or a PPF (7%), or a MF (say, 12%).
- Now play around with time, changing the duration for shorter or longer. Think of scenarios, products, interest rates, changing time horizons.

Why are we doing this?

To get a feel of how money shrinks or grows in different scenarios, and how much of a difference consistency over time makes.

Also, I want you to get used to playing with Excel. It's going to be critical - and the more comfortably you can run the numbers for any evaluation, the better you'll be at judging the long-term impact of your decisions.

. . .

CHAPTER IV

Risk & Reward

Returns are on a spectrum, ranging from low-risk / low-reward, to high-risk / high-reward.

This means some financial products will give a low return, but they will always give a low return, (*under most situations.*) They're stable, reliable, dependable. You can expect them to be there, with that same return, at any planned time in future. They're safe.

Others will give a very high return, but - and this is very important - not all the time. Some years they can give huge returns, far exceeding what you expected. Other years, that performance drops. Reduces, goes to less than the safe options, to zero, sometimes even to negative. Later, it may come back again... or it may never recover.

And you cannot reliably predict *when* this will happen.

Every financial investment product falls somewhere on this range.

This is the fundamental nature of financial products; there's very little you can do to change their nature, except choosing those that work for you.

But as you choose, spread out your money over the spectrum, so you balance *some* low-risk (*keeping money safe, but growing slowly, or not at all*) vs *some* higher-risk (*a chance to grow money faster than inflation, but with the risk that sometimes, it could also go low, even zero.*)

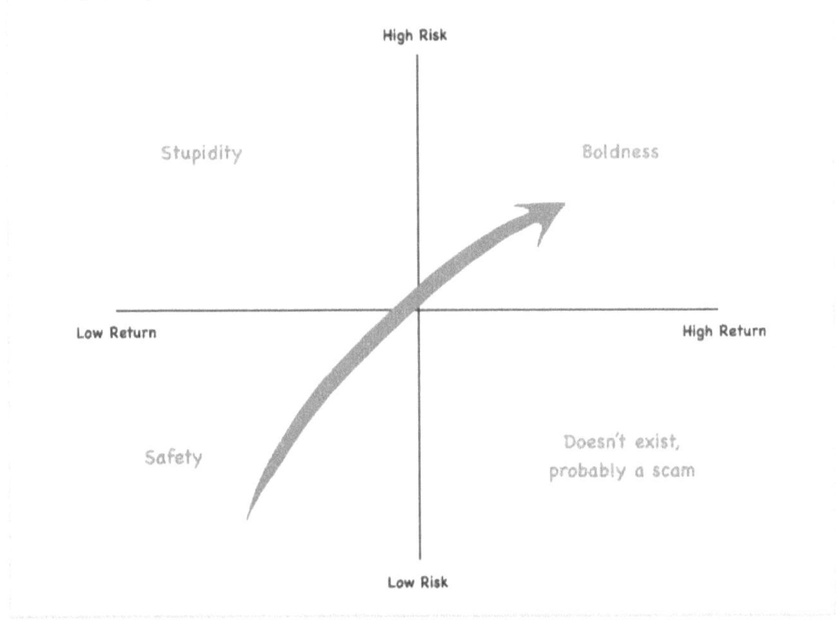

Risk v/s Reward

Going ahead, I'll talk about options along this spectrum, from basics, to safe options, and then gradually increasing the risk-and-reward level. You'll have to choose where along the line you're comfortable going, and how much of your earnings you put in play at each stage.

Start with safe options, because that's the foundation and the fallback plan. If catastrophe hits, this is the baseline where you want to land up; the security of survival, knowing you at least won't be out on the street. Then, gradually move towards riskier ones, because while staying safe all your life might keep you off the streets, it's still just one step above the street. You aspire to the big bang, sky-high lifestyle, so you're going to have to take some risks to get there.

In life, as your financial situation changes, you'll need to move back and forth on the line as well. Staying 100% safe, all the time, means missing out on critical opportunities; but going 100% risky, all the time, will in the long run inevitably put you in a situation where you lose everything.

Why's it like this? Because of human nature. Everyone wants safety, but if everyone's doing it, the rewards also spread out to far too many people, and get diluted. If you do something that very few people do, the rewards can be much more - but there's also a reason few people do it.

Because few survive it.

Is taking risks stupid, then?

No, not if you know what you're doing - which means not just being different from everyone else, but also doing that hard work of learning, researching, upskilling, being able to understand how each financial product works, what affects it, and being sufficiently aware of what's happening in the world to make an educated guess about how any financial product might perform.

If you don't do this hard work, then you're really just doing wishful thinking... **and taking stupid risks.**

How much risk should you take?

A basic thumb rule is - for every 100 rupees you invest, put (*100 minus your current age*)% in *relatively* riskier (with higher potential reward) places.

Why? Because the younger you are, the less dependents, less responsibilities you have - making recovery from mistakes easier, and you have more time in which to recover. Making mistakes with smaller amounts early is better than big mistakes later.

And if done early enough, even a small win can compound into a big one over time. And you have time.

Then older you get, the more serious the consequences of mistakes get - so you should start moving towards safer bets with age, and protect your hard-earned returns.

• • •

To Do

- Make a list of 10-15 possible investment options. They can be anything you like, from super safe to stupidly risky, but should be legitimate (*i.e. no manufacturing & selling hard drugs*) and available to you.
- For each one, lookup and list the top 3-5 pros and cons. Pros will usually be along earnings, flexibility, stability, protection, and safety, but the cons will be interesting - that's where you'll get the sense of what risks are associated with each one.
- ChatGPT, (*or Gemini, or Copilot, or whatever else is the preferred AI whenever you're reading this*) can be a very helpful tool to use here, because you can do a deeper dive into concepts you don't immediately get.
- Do you understand each risk?
- Draw the above 2X2 chart.
- Can you fit each option in the correct quadrant?

Remember, not all risks are linked with the financial instrument alone. You can always lose credentials or passwords, be stuck in inheritance bureaucracy, get scammed by an unscrupulous 3rd party pretending to sell a legit option, identity theft, etc. For this exercise, though, let's try to judge the options on their inherent features and merits.

• • •

CHAPTER V

Fear and Greed

The two reasons why everyone does *anything* with money.

And both these reasons are very prone to misinformation, hype, media frenzy, rumor, market panic, scams, hearsay and gossip, because the more scary - or attractive - something is, the more people like to talk about it... So the more you hear about it.

Fear is when you back off, decide not to invest, or pull out of an investment. It's a healthy response, because it's keeping you safe, but it can have the negative effect of stopping you from doing anything at all. Remember, there's no such thing as perfect safety - banks can fail, houses can get robbed, tax rules can get changed.

Fear can also cause losses, when you get pulled into a panic, and get out of an investment before time; this is why panic sellers always lose money. Many higher-risk instruments are volatile, because they are affected by the world. If you don't know what's happening, and have only your emotions to base your actions on, then your own fear response will prematurely pull you back.

Another, different, side of fear is **FOMO - the fear of missing out.** If all your friends seem to be doing fantastically well, you'll be tempted to ape in - and without understanding what you're doing, you'll make mistakes, so many mistakes. Then, you'll panic and get out, leaving all your potential rewards behind.

Greed is the opposite - you get so caught up with what you think the rewards are going to be, you miss, or ignore, all the red flags and warning signs. Lost in dreams of the fancy car and big house, you become the perfect target for scams, frauds, and bad advice.

Greed is what criminals and scammers prey on, because it overwrites and short-circuits rational thought - *especially* when rational thought is saying, '*something doesn't smell right.*'

When that happens, you'll hate rational thought, because it seems to be trying to stop you from getting what you so desperately want. Don't. Even though it's not a feel-good action, face that sense of disquiet, *examine* it in detail. Is there a logical reason why you feel you should be more careful? Does it look too good to be true? Has anyone else done this, that you know of, independently? Is the guy selling this legit?

Get greedy, and end up not only without the expected reward, but also potentially lose all what you invested.

• • •

So how do you overcome these emotions?

Decouple from emotional decisions, by *making them rule-based.*

- Checklist #1: Is the *source* legitimate? When planning to buy any investment, is the seller or company's credentials, capabilities and legitimacy verifiable? Are they listed or accredited on 3rd party sources? Has anyone else worked with them in depth, over time?
- Checklist #2: Is the *investment option* legitimate? How long has it been in existence, how many people have heard of it, is it regulated, are there defined, publicly available data points that can be used to check the quality? Is it an only one-of-a-kind, or can you compare options? Is the amount affordable? Can you track performance? What are the exit criteria, process, time, and fees?
- Checklist #3: Is the *timing* right? Can you validate if you are buying into a hype bubble, where everyone is either running from or away from an option just because of social media, news, or rumors? Are you buying at the all-time high, or selling at the low, because that's when it makes the most news? Is there an artificial high or low because of market sentiment or global situation?
- Checklist #4: Opportunity cost. What can you do, *instead of this?* Are you risking losing out on a bigger better opportunity, or some other critical payment, by putting in money here?

It's hard to do, and often this information isn't 100% available - but asking a few of these basic questions can filter out a lot of potential dangers. Don't worry, as you start doing this, you'll get better and better, until this becomes an unconscious habit.

• • •

To Do

Pick any 2 different investment options, and examine them for both Fear and Greed.

Is there a sense of nervousness or discomfort? Or the opposite, are you finding yourself fervently wishing for a good outcome and seeing dreams more than facts?

Draw up 5 (objective, data-based) conditions to decide if -

- The person you're buying from is legit
- The investment itself is ok
- Are the goals realistic, and what do they depend on?
- Is it currently at a high or low? Do you know why?
- What are you taking money away from, by buying this? How does it compare?

The objective is not to make a checklist now, but a *mental training exercise* in moving away from that emotional, 'I really want this' or 'I really should get out of this,' self-convincing state of mind, to *a more objective approach*. Once you start doing this, for every new or potential option that comes along, it'll become second nature.

Don't completely discount emotional triggers, though. Sometimes your mind can *subconsciously* make connections you may not be aware of, and the result is a strong emotional trigger. Doing an objective exercise also allows you to validate your feelings, and identify if something needs to be checked out more.

It's slow and painful, but that's the point. If you want fast and fun, catch a Rohit Shetty movie.

• • •

CHAPTER VI

Diversification

A 100% of anything is bad. You've got to have a decent mix of different things to get the best of all, and balance out.

A farmer works dawn to dusk all his life, and ends up with a tough, but satisfying, life. (*Low risk, low reward*).

A rebel leader, who tries to take the throne *sometimes* becomes king (*high reward*), but *usually* ends up dead, or imprisoned. (*High risk*).

But in between these, there's a range of things you can do, that could give a better life than either one of these approaches.

This means you need to spread out your efforts, attention, and earnings, across a variety of products, and also across a variety of components within each product, where possible.

Different products are affected by different factors. It could be the state of the economy, laws, import and export, new technology, monetary policy, supply and demand, popular culture, the weather, geopolitics, local politics, social trends, even the individual actions of a big company's CEO, or a political leader. All these have their own cycles - i.e. they tend to repeat patterns at different rates - and they all affect, and interact, with each other.

Which means sometimes, several factors coincidentally line up together, and an entire sector or category of products will do exceptionally well - or really badly. If you're smart, you can hazard a guess at what factors are playing a part and when, and try to profit - but with so many random factors involved, it's pretty much impossible (*unless the change is so huge, it can override a lot of other influences.*)

For example - in good economic conditions, smaller companies have a chance to do well, so can give really good returns. If times are bad, these same small companies are more likely to go bust, while the bigger ones have the resources to sustain themselves, and do relatively less badly. If you were all-in on only small companies, and times turned bad, you could lose everything. And if these bad times happened at a point when you *really* needed to cash out - a wedding, retirement, some emergency - you'd have no choice, but to sell out at those low prices.

Instead, if you have a *mix* of *different* financial instruments, spread across different sectors and sizes, it would bring overall stability - as one lot goes down, it's balanced by others going up. If you ever needed cash in an emergency, there would always be *something* in your portfolio that hasn't lost all its value, (or has gained) and can be cashed out, while the temporarily poor performers can be retained, in expectation of better times ahead.

This is how you *protect* your money. Later, when times get good once more, others that were doing badly start to pick up again, and you can re-adjust your mix.

• • •

To Do

- List everything you have your money invested in, in broad categories. Bank accounts, PPFs, FD if any, Mutual funds, Equity, etc.
- List the amount against each.
- Is there any single one that is much bigger than the others... like more than half?

If the answer is yes, then you have a diversification problem. *Too many eggs in one basket.*

- Repeat the exercise, if you can, with the sub-components inside each - say, inside equities, can you break down by market cap or sector?

You don't need to jump into making dramatic changes *right* away - but it's important that you *recognize* this disbalanced situation exists, and pay attention to planning how it will need to change going forward. It's an indicator that your current investing pattern is skewed one way, more than others, for some reason - can you figure out what's influencing you like this?

As we go through the rest of this book, we'll see multiple things that need to be done; you'll need to keep adding onto your mix of financial instruments and options, to keep them evolving over time.

The point of doing this *now* is to establish a baseline - where are you starting out from? What needs to be given a greater weightage in future, to achieve overall balance?

• • •

CHAPTER VII

Paycheck-to-Paycheck

A situation where all the money earned in a month (typically from salary) is *completely* used in that month, with *nothing left over* for savings. This is a very dangerous situation to be in, because -

- If salary stops (layoffs, firings), your needs will not - and there'll be no way to pay for them.
- Any increase in needs or wants can't be sustained, as it exceeds available money.
- There's no opportunity to upskill or build a better career / business, because you have no available time and resources; you can't take a break to study, build a business, or even take a side course.
- An emergency is a disaster - with no emergency fund, you'll have to take loans to manage, which then becomes another drain on your cash flow as you repay them.
- And forget about taking a sabbatical or a mental-health break.

Instead, if you were able to save even a little each month, over time that adds up to a reserve that can handle emergencies, sustain you during unemployed times, and maybe give you a little cushion for some extra spending.

Living paycheck to paycheck also leaves you *super* vulnerable to inflation, because -

If you earn just enough to pay for every need, even a small increase in cost for everything will push you over budget, and into debt. Debt's even more expensive than inflation, so you sink further in the hole; it's a vicious circle, and you keep getting buried deeper and deeper.

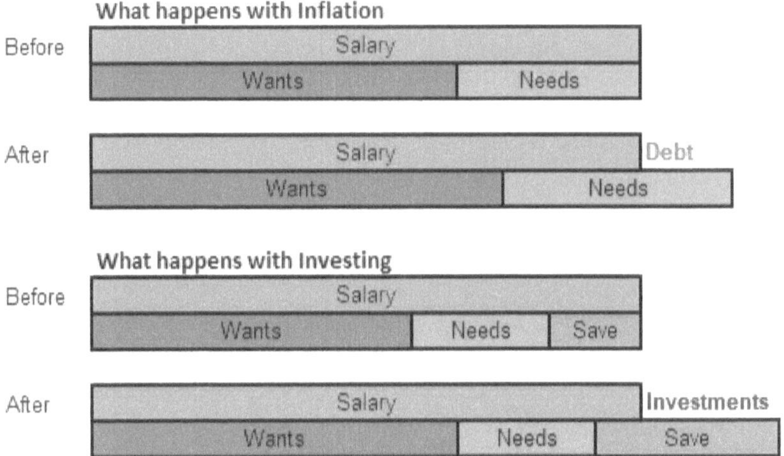

Paycheck to Paycheck: Risks

But if you earn even a little more than what you need, then that small increase in price can't hurt you immediately. You have time to adjust. And if this extra money is being invested, and giving a return greater than inflation, then your total income is also increasing more than inflation!

You're not only out of the hole, but actually rising higher.

• • •

To Do

This one's an easy exercise.

- At the end of the month, once you've paid everyone, bought everything, and spent all you needed - how much is still left?
- If the answer is negative, zero, or negligible, keep going. You'll need the next few chapters.
- If the answer is a decent positive sum, congratulations! You've got a good hold on life.
- **Keep going anyway.**

. . .

CHAPTER VIII

Taxes

Again, an easy concept, but *surprisingly* easy to forget in the heat of the moment.

Every gain, every income, is taxed. And since pretty much *all* investment vehicles are KYC-mandatory, and linked to your PAN and identity, the I-T dept usually will have a very clear idea of *exactly* how much you're making... and how much you should be paying.

The problem comes when you -

a) make your plans and decisions in evaluating what investments to do, and

b) actually make that profit, and either reinvest back (*good child!*) or spend it,

c) forget that a chunk (12.5% - 40%, depending on tax bracket) of that profit belongs to the I-T dept... and come July, *they're going to collect.*

Apart from simply forgetting we owe tax on our profits as a general concept, we also mess up on the *specifics* of that payment.

We forget that some investments get taxed more than others; eg. long-term vs short-term, and not factoring in the actual taxes that are going to be applied, we misjudge the real returns, i.e. what you actually made, in hand, after paying your taxes.

Eg - Say, all you had to invest was Rs. 1,00,000, the goal was retirement, and you chose the simple 10% MF over the 8% NPS. You actually lost out - because the 10K you made from the MF will be reduced by 3K going in taxes, while the 8K NPS return was tax free. Another reason to make sure you focus on the tax savings first.

Sometimes, we cash out. Some investment hits a target value, we sell, celebrate the 50% profit we made, rush out and buy whatever we were waiting for. We forget that come tax season, there'll be a 20-30% tax applied on that 50% return! The I-T dept won't care if you've already spent it on your holiday, your party, or your boy/girlfriend. You're going have to cough it up, and if you hadn't considered it and set a part aside, you're going to be *squeezed* hard for a while. Not a pleasant experience... and very disruptive for any kind of post-July planning.

For added complexity, tax slabs change rates with income level, regime rules are different, regulations can change. One of the nastiest shocks you can experience is getting an increment that put you into a higher tax bracket - it's possible to raise the CTC and lose the take-home. It's important to understand, before starting out, some core aspects of your income and how it relates to the tax rules.

$$\bullet \ \bullet \ \bullet$$

To Do

- What's your total income - gross CTC, before taxes?
- Does that include income from interest, dividends, and other returns? How much is that?
- How much of that falls into the taxable category? (i.e. after removing allowed deductions, expenses, and tax saver contributions)
- What is the tax rate per slab, and which one are you in?
- Can you put a rough estimate, basis the above and planned investments, what amount of your returns will need to be paid out in taxes?
- Can you park an X % (basis your understanding of the effective tax slabs) out of each return or dividend aside, towards a future tax payment? (*Yes, income tax is deducted, but only from your salary*)

Again, this may not be relevant to a lot of people early on, especially if their investments are at relatively low levels - but since you're here, reading this - the expectation is that sooner rather than later, you'll be making a decent little pile of cash over and above the basic salary, right?

• • •

CHAPTER IX

Intermission 1

Harsh stares into the glaring screen. A neat black-and-white column of figures. In the dark living-room, it's enough even at the lowest brightness, to burn a mocking, floating afterimage before him, wherever he turns his head or shuts his eyes.

His almost-daily headache which started as a mild twinge in the early evenings, is now a hard, pulsing drum. He really ought to sleep, he knows - in a few hours he's got to be up again, a quick, quiet breakfast to avoid waking the baby, and be alert enough to manage the hour-long, terrifyingly-fast, early morning traffic through grey fog and wet roads to work.

But he can't look away.

All the struggling, the effort, the sacrifice - it comes down to this little column.

The 'big' number on top, which friends back home translated with currency conversion rates, giving awed, envious whistles, while he grinned and nodded proudly... saying nothing.

The slowly-shrinking figures marching down, as life happened.

Rent. Credit cards. Mandatory insurance. Bills. Fuel. Food.

He remembers, once - surprisingly not that long ago - there was travel. Movies. Eating out. Gifts. Sending money home.

Even saving.

It's been over two years since he met his parents face-to-face. To compensate, he's tried the regular videocalling route... but it would inevitably end with the same questions he couldn't answer anymore, over and over.

When are you coming? Why not? I don't understand...

He calls less and less these days, and he can feel the hurt across continents.

What can he do, though? They don't know the reality, just like he once didn't, years ago. They only look big. The big life they promised was a lie.

The numbers get smaller and smaller. Pharmacy. Formula, diapers. Repairs.

He's moved twice now into poorer neighborhoods, smaller apartments, trying to stay ahead of the inevitable rent hikes. He's driving longer, spending more and more time on the road, less at home.

Weekends are an exhausting, empty space staring blankly into the TV, or the inevitable arguments. Roshni has gone from bright vivacity to a shadow of herself, gaunt and quiet, and even their fights slide quickly from angry shouts to bitter silences.

It's better to pick up Uber rides, or just go to work instead - maybe that overtime will count towards the next promotion or raise.

Even if it hasn't, the last three years. This year could be the one.

Smaller. Late fees. Overdraft charges. A speeding ticket.

He can't give up now. What was it all for? The studying, the loans, the plans, the hopes and dreams...

Ironically, it's that time that feels like a dream now. Maybe this, tonight, is the nightmare, and he'll wake up soon. His visa renewal's due, and there's rumors of layoffs coming. If the worst happens... how'll he look anyone in the face again?

His eyes reluctantly slide down to the last number, and this one's red as blood. The blood that drips from a thousand small cuts of those inescapable expenses. It's gone below that waterline where he could still keep his head above water, so to say. Balance income to expense.

Negative. In the red.

He has nothing left, less than nothing. Whatever he could do, he's done.

But... there's always tomorrow.

He gently shuts the laptop, rubs his eyes, and leans back in the dark. One exhausted tear trickles into his early-grey hairline.

A wordless prayer, to a nameless entity, hopelessly offered in silence.

Please. Anything.

A job offer, with visa sponsorship. A raise, a promotion. Even just a generous tip.

Nobody answers, nothing happens. He knows better. Life doesn't work like that anymore.

But he still hopes.

It could still all be ok. Something could work out.

Tomorrow.

• • •

CHAPTER X

Structuring a Personal Finance Journey

So, now that you have the critical concepts in your head, let's lay out a plan for how we're going to tackle this.

Like I said earlier, there're a *lot* of different books out there on finance. They can be super focused and specialized in a topic; broad encyclopedias; general reading for basic concepts; even philosophical social treatises, and many more.

The question you're struggling with - given all this information available, *what do I do first?*

• • •

I'm going to define a structure, an approach for how to set up your personal finance.

My goal's to build a basic conceptual skeleton of the critical basics, on top of which you can select and apply specific choices depending on your situation and goals. Those specifics are going to be up to you - it's dependent on every person's own particular situation, preferences, constraints and mindset.

I don't know what that is, for you.

Only *you* know.

Therefore, only *you* are going to choose.

But this basic skeleton, the foundation, is meant to make sure the critical components have been covered, done in a sequence that allows you to build up a clear and complete picture of what you're doing, where different financial instruments and choices fit in, how it affects your life and plans, and perhaps, exposes some existing gaps or mistakes that can be fixed.

My approach is -

- Define methods to get control of what's going on, today
- Understand where your money comes from, and where it goes
- Identify a starting point
- Prepare for the critical, potentially catastrophic, points of failure
- Cover up for the danger areas that can derail the whole journey
- Plan for a baseline, fallback option (*a Plan B*) in case disaster does strike

- Show how to grow your money on top of all this
- Set and target end goals.

In between, I'll be adding ideas on other, related concepts.

This isn't a what-to-do list, but an open discussion - here's what *I* think. How about *you*?

Through all this, I will *not* recommend a single stock, financial instrument, website, news source, book, person, or course. The point of this book is to build good financial habits, and the first thing for that is to be independent, educated, curious, experimentative - and above all, responsible.

Never listen to, or follow, someone blindly.

So once you have this mental structure in place, you'll be able to -

- See what you need to focus on first;
- Identify what type of financial product or investment (or other actions) you need to take;
- Have a sense of how to evaluate if a financial product is relevant or useful to you or not.

If that works, let's go ahead.

• • •

How to DYOR

I've mentioned the need to do your own research several times, so let me also outline how to approach it without getting lost.

1. Start with general books, or a beginner level course (*on Udemy, LinkedIn, or similar.*) You just need one that talks about broad concepts.
2. Keep an AI window open (*or Wikipedia, Google, or similar*) where you can pause and quickly lookup details of a topic. An AI (*eg. ChatGPT, Perplexity, Copilot, Gemini, etc*) are preferred because you can have a two-way conversation to clarify anything you didn't quite get.
3. Search up topics on Youtube. Do NOT follow influencers who promise tips and what-to-do, without talking about how-to-do.
4. Test and track. Set up accounts, practice. Keep a track of what you're doing, why, and what you expect to happen. Having this recorded makes it easier to understand when you were right, or why you were wrong.
5. Now you have enough basic awareness to get into more specialist areas and topics
6. Talk to a professional. Get their perspective and opinion, as long as it's based on experience and expertise.

    1. If you understand and agree, your learning's valid.
    2. If you understand and disagree, debate. Find out why you disagree.
    3. If you don't understand, listen. Go back and learn more.

• • •

A Personal Finance Journey - Visualization

- Visualize your goals - why are you here?
- Understand your cash flow - where is your money coming from, and going?
- Prepare for emergencies
- Get out of debt - stop your money bleeding away
- Build a saving habit for short-term goals
- Learn to invest for long-term goals with different products
- Revisit and update the plan regularly.

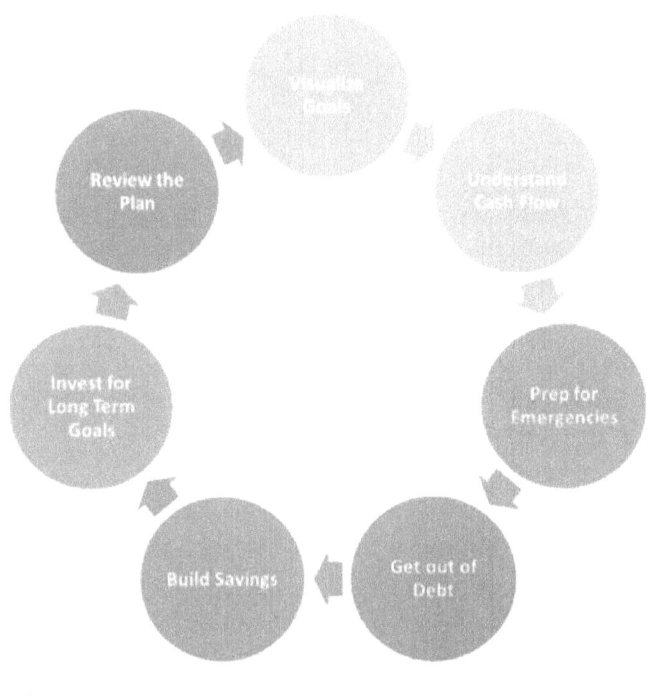

• • •

Imagine your life.

Not as it is today, but look both back and forth, past and future, and try to build a picture in your head of what it's been, and how you'd like it to be.

The Past -

What are the strengths your background has given you - education, awareness, a network of contacts, specific skills, any material advantages - an inheritance, a home, a business, a job?

What are the weaknesses?

What's missing, what you wish you had? Are there past incidents that feel uncomfortable, act as a mental block for how you think about money?

What are your fears and your desires around money, and why do you think you have them?

Why do you want to manage your money better? And what might be stopping you?

This is an important step, because it will guide how you go forward... and help you understand why you are reluctant, or enthused, to adopt certain approaches or take some actions, and not others.

The Future -

Starting from right now, visualize what comes next, in broad swathes of time - say, five-year blocks. The first 5-10 years will be easy, because you're already looking at them, and have some plans. It'll get murkier after, as you never had need, or reason, to think of them so soon.

The problem with this short-term visual, is you'll end up planning only for the next 5-10 years; and at any point of time, you'll only be able to benefit from the planning of the last 5-10 years.

Doing this exercise will *expand your time horizon.*

Don't worry - we're not going to jump straight into saving for events decades in the future. But, we will build an appreciation for the fact that these events exist, and will come.

And the longer we have to prepare, the better prepared we'll be.

The point of doing that, is to -

- Understand that as we build habits of saving, we're saving for goals beyond the immediate time (and mental) horizon
- Appreciate that we cannot predict the future and build a 100% perfect foolproof plan. We need to build something that has a long-term validity, but is also flexible to accommodate changes and twists in the road.

Now, to stop this staying a mere imagination exercise, let's put this to paper. List out key events you expect to occur in each life bloc, and what would be the expected financial impact of these.

For example, it might look a little like this -

Time Bloc	My Age	Activities	Cost	Prep time
1-5 years	25	Fix basic planning Move out of parents home	5L	5 years
5-10 years	30	Get married Emigration	20L	10 years
10-15 years	35	Have 1-2 kids Executive education Buy a car 10-year Anniv holiday	30L	15 years
15-20 years	40	Kids School admissions Buy a house	1Cr	20 years
20-25 years	45	Parents health issues Own business Support dependents	2Cr	25 years
25-30 years	50	Kids higher education	50L	30 years
30-35 years	55	Long-term dream goal	25L	35 years
35-40 years	60	Kids marriages	50L	40 years
40-45 years	65	Retirement, income gone	1Cr	45 years
45-50 years	70	Health issues	75L	50 years
50-55 years	75	Health issues	50L	55 years
55-60 years	80	Death	25L	60 years

A Rough Life Plan

Sigh. *That's* depressing.
Your life in a 12-row excel sheet.

• • •

Remember, this is indicative. It's not a recommendation on how your, or anyone's, life is supposed to go. *You* need to draw up *your* own plan for life. Stuff will move around, get knocked off, change order... but there *will* be major events, and they will be of such a size and scale, that you *cannot* just put them on a credit card (*even with zero-cost EMI options!*)

You have to visualize this to understand, as we move to goal planning later, *what are the goals you want - and what you need to do to get them.*

Now, here's another depressing fact.

The amounts above are practically meaningless - I've added them to only make a point. Actual reality will be very different, dependent on what's happened, happening, and expected to.

Also, the amounts here are based on guesswork, at today's rates. Ten years on, things will be much more expensive, and will keep getting more so. Remember, inflation? You'll need to come back to this sheet, and adjust the rates accordingly.

• • •

But wait, there's more!

What we've talked about has been a *perfect* life.

> *Everybody has a plan until they get punched in the mouth.*
>
> *- Mike Tyson*

So, let's go ahead, and get punched in the mouth.

As players of strategy games are (*painfully*) aware, it's easy to build a perfect ecosystem, with enough time and planning. What makes the game *interesting* is the random disasters that get thrown at you from time to time, completely disrupting everything and wrecking your perfect run.

Let's choose any 3 disasters.

This will get a little dark, but bear with me. Not thinking about bad things gives them power - when they happen, we can't handle them because we have no idea how to think about them, let alone having a plan.

It's ok to think about potential disasters - it isn't morbid, and doesn't invite them into your life. But also don't obsess over them constantly, because that way lies madness.

Pick any 3 of the below, and add them to your life plan, at random places. The randomness is important - don't expect them to happen when you want. They'll happen when *they* want. Switch them around periodically, and see if it's still manageable.

3 is a decent number - too many more, you might want to get checked for curses, and less, you're being a little too optimistic.

1. *I crashed my car, broke my leg. Hospital for a week. Cannot go to office for 6 months.*
2. *My company shut down, and I got laid off.*
3. *My visa got revoked, and I was deported.*
4. *I clicked on a link I shouldn't have, and everything in my bank account is gone.*
5. *My house was robbed! All my jewellery, cash, and electronics are gone!*
6. *War was declared, and my house was was bombed into rubble.*
7. *A global pandemic forced me to shut down my business.*
8. *Cancer.*
9. *My spouse left me and moved out. Half the household income is gone as well.*
10. *I have been named and penalized in a legal case for damages.*
11. *Everyone was given a 40% salary cut without warning to keep the company alive.*

12. *My bank / investment collapsed in a scam when the owners ran off with all deposits.*

13. *The under-construction house I bought, has got stuck in litigation and may never be completed.*

And so on, so forth. Any of these can happen, mostly at any time. When they happen, it can be hellishly expensive... but also disorienting, throwing everything out of gear, and upending regular life-as-usual. As much as the cost of handling it, you'll also need to prepare *mentally*.

• • •

Now, before we begin...

Let's take a moment and understand where we are. Reader, you're here, this book in your hand, because you had some idea that you want to do better in handling your finances - but how much trouble are you actually in? How much help do you need?

To answer that, let's do a quick **quiz**.

- *Right now, are you -*

  - *Having life insurance with coverage of at least a year?*
  - *Able to handle a sudden emergency, costing half your monthly salary?*
  - *Having more than 1 EMI running with over 3 years to go?*
  - *Wanting to buy X, but have no idea when, and how, you can afford it?*

- *Each month, do you -*

  - *Get into fights over money, the last 10 days of the month?*
  - *Know roughly how much you're spending, and where?*
  - *Know what bills are due, when, and for approximately how much?*
  - *Ask for tips on what stocks to buy or sell?*

- *In the last year, did you -*

  - *Make a part-payment on your CC more than once, paid a late fee?*
  - *Wait for a bonus to pay some critical expense?*
  - *Commit to some recurring investment, just because someone told you to?*
  - *Get surprised by an unexpected bill, or tax, and struggled to pay?*

If you answered 'yes' 4 times or more... welcome. You're in the right place - the rest that follows, if we work together, will be helpful in getting control of your personal finances and fixing some of the burning issues.

If you said mostly 'no',congratulations - you seem to be well in control of your finances. The rest of the book can be an opportunity to validate your approach, find ways to fine-tune and improve it - and I'd love to hear your inputs on what you did to get here!

• • •

To Do
Storage of critical documents

- Set a **private physical** location, a **public physical** location, and a **digital** location.

What's that?

- The **private physical location** needs to be *safe, secure, and inaccessible* - a locked desk drawer or cupboard, or later, a safe. This should contain the important, irreplaceable documents -
- Original passport, identity documents, birth certificates, marriage certificates, death certificates
- Deeds and ownership documents, authenticity certificates, original investment proofs
- Original insurance documents
- Original education certificates
- A backup medium containing digital versions of key documents, updated periodically
- Will (if you made one)
- Physical passbooks for investment schemes and retirement accounts

The **public physical location** needs to be in a *safe and secure* place in your house, *not out in the open, but accessible to anyone who needs it.* Eg. A dedicated shelf in an unlocked cupboard or large desk drawer, a good box under your bed. The location and its contents *should be known to your spouse or any other responsible adults,* but not children or domestic staff. In this you will store -

- Tax documents - Form-16, tax challans and ITRs
- Salary slips and joining letters
- Copies of Lease or Home Ownership paperwork
- Copies of Identity documents - Aadhar, PAN, passport, birth certificates
- Copies of education certificates and qualifications
- Insurance premium receipts
- Recent utility bills (up to a year)
- Medical records and reports
- Receipts and warranties of high-value items

- Tickets, visas

The **digital location** should be ideally a **cloud-based one** (*like Dropbox or Drive*), and contain *scans* of the key documents held in both physical locations. The purpose of this is to ensure easy access to often-required docs that can be printed / copied if required from any place, without having to keep accessing (and risking) originals, plus serve as a reference point if any data point needs to be looked up.

It should be -

- Password protected or encrypted
- Shared with critical responsible adults only
- Not enabled for offline access or backed up locally, unless that is also encrypted / protected (in case you lose your phone / laptop)
- Backed up onto a physical USB or drive at least once a year and stored in the secure physical location (in case the storage service closes down)

• • •

Your Personal Finance Journey Checklist

Use this to track your progress. It's sequential, interlinked, and we'll come back to it as we move on.

You'll see this page again & again. That's not a mistake - it's *supposed* to be there, because as you go, you'll need to check if you're on the right track, and can see progress not just with page count, but with the skills & abilities needed.

I have -

- Decided to take control of my personal finances
- Allocated a dedicated storage area for my documentation
- Understood the basic concepts of inflation, compounding, and risk
- Made a monthly budget, and follow it
- Familiarized myself with my salary structure and all benefits
- Purchased life insurance with payout of at least a year's earning
- Purchased personal health insurance with all critical riders
- Set up an emergency fund of at least 3 months' income
- Automated standard bill payments
- Cleared all my outstanding credit card and high-interest debts
- Reduced regular debts to under 30% of income
- Started contributing to a functional retirement account
- Utilized fully the tax saver components of my salary
- Deployed goal-based RDs
- Saved in at least one long-term FD
- Created a diversified mutual fund portfolio
- Invested in a diversified equity portfolio
- Explored 1-2 alternative investments
- Secured my digital footprint and credentials
- Started researching alternative income streams
- Planned the regular biannual physical checkup
- Vacationed at least once a year
- Reviewed each of the above in detail every 5 years.

• • •

45

Income

*Most people work just hard enough not to get fired, and get paid just enough
money not to quit.*

George Carlin

CHAPTER XI

Budgeting

Dull, boring, painful.
Who cares when you spend what?
Why you have to make list... rent, bills, fees, food, all that? How much, when, to who?

Impossible. Always you forget something. All work goes for toss, waste of time, panic for no reason.

Why worry from before?
You have money, you pay whatever when it comes.
When money is over, pay next month.

Don't stress. Problem for future.
You can always get money later, right?

See - if you spend more than you get, then that is motivation to earn more. Makes brain work faster, to get more money.

And if you not paying, some people giving up, going away. Problem solved!

• • •

I moved to Mumbai back in 2002, looking for work. Not being from the city, I needed a place to live while I hunted for jobs; also not being employed, this had to be cheap. This meant a shared apartment deep in the dug-up, traffic-choked, narrow-lane suburbs shared with 5 other guys, and the owner using the living room as his design office.

Once a month, each of us would give our share of the rent, in cash, to one of us who'd hand it over to the owner. That rent was all-inclusive, covering stay, electricity, bike parking, twice-a-week cleaning, and access to a mini-kitchen. Matter closed.

Anyone who didn't pay, would first lose his deposit, then get evicted. **Simple, straightforward, no-fuss.** We'd each subscribe individually for dabba service on weekdays, and eat out as a group on weekends, splitting the bill in cash. This was almost an exact replica of the last few years' hostel life, and I adjusted to it immediately.

Then, a year later, I moved into a rented apartment with a roommate... and suddenly the cash situation got more *complex*. Rent had to be paid, by check, from a single bank account. Electricity, cable, internet, and cleaners were charged separately, but consumed between us; we had individual phones and laptops, but stuff like a TV, washing machine, microwave, even food orders, etc were shared buys. Now, it was no longer as easy as putting an X amount in a common pool, and being done.

So, I started writing down the shared expenses in a notebook.

Who had paid for what, and how much, and when. End of the month, we'd add up our individual contribs, and split the difference. This went on for a while... the notebook started getting ragged, and falling apart; so I switched to an excel sheet.

And once I was on Excel, just for timepass and practice, I started tracking spend over time, identifying categories, and looking at past patterns and projecting ahead, predicting future cash flow requirements. The sheets would start simple, get complicated, get overcomplicated and cumbersome, then be cut back to critical data again. Each cycle, I'd learn a little bit more about my behavior, needs, habits, constraints, problems, and solutions.

Later on, I'd move into my own place, get married, start saving - but the basic process, of *simply recording where the money was going*, remained the core of staying on top of my personal finances.

Oh, there were *plenty* of mistakes made along the way. Bonuses would get blown up. Insurance premiums and credit-card bills would come as a sudden shock, be delayed, penalties charged. There'd be sudden, unexpected large purchases and spends. But every time something happened that broke the process, just by adding it to the record, it would become a part of the process.

Almost from first principles, I'd discovered a form of budgeting that worked for my situation.

That was the starting point for me. I didn't realize then, just what a powerful tool it was - but having that visibility over what I was spending, allowed me to control it, direct it, and gave me a framework onto which other financial tools could be fitted.

Just like that, for you too, it all needs to start from Budgeting.

It's literally **Step Zero.** The *first* thing you have to do.

If controlling your money is a war, then a budget is a map of the battlefield. Without a budget, you're just running around in the dark, waiting for the enemy to come out of nowhere, and kill you.

• • •

But budgeting doesn't have to be hard, or complex.

Just follow these steps.

- Open an excel sheet (paper and pencil is also fine, if you prefer)
- I assume you get your salary on the 1ˢᵗ of the month. Write that down. *1/1/24 | Salary | 50,000*
- **Make a list** of all the things where that salary gets spent, starting with the largest. Rent? Credit card payments? EMIs? Salary paid to *bai?* Bills? Groceries? Petrol? Fees? Repairs? Returning borrowed money? Stocks? Try to cover all the major ones - doesn't have to be 100% of every small thing, but at least reach 90% of the big ones. It'll take a couple of tries, the first few months, to work out the details.
- Next to each item, put the **date** it has to be paid, and the **amount.** You'll have a rough idea how much this is in most cases; If not, a few months of doing this will give you that clarity. Remember to cross-check against reality - what was the actual amount?

Date	Item	Amount
01/01/24	Rent	18,000
05/01/24	Car EMI	6,000
10/01/24	CC Bill	6,000
02/01/24	Food	6,000
10/01/24	Bills	2,000
03/01/24	Maid	6,000
10/01/24	Travel	2,000
15/01/24	Entertainment	2,000
25/01/24	Savings	2,000

List the dates, items, & amounts

- Against each item, mark the item as **'Need'**, **'Save'**, and **'Want'**.

    Some items might need to be separated - an electricity bill is a need, but a Netflix subscription is a want. Feel free to break up items like this, but avoid getting too granular right now, keep it simple.

A '**Save**' is something that makes no difference to you today, but can have a *big impact later* - PPF, mutual funds, etc.
Don't touch this yet, we'll come back to it.Even if it's zero, keep it as an entry.
This category is your flag, your king piece in the budget war. It *has* to be defended. If you lose *this*, you've lost the game.

A '**Need**' is something that you *have* to do - rent, EMIs, electricity bill, taxes, etc. If you don't pay this, *bad* things happen, very quickly - like fines, no power, and getting thrown out on the street.

A '**Want**' is *optional* stuff - holidays, shopping, subscriptions, restaurants, etc. If you stop or reduce this, life still goes on, albeit a *little* different. A 'want' isn't affected by how much you like it - you might *think* you must eat out or order in from a good restaurant, every alternate day, but you won't die eating that basic homemade food.
- Group your list into these 3 areas, in that order. **Total it up.**
This basic budgeting is going to be an activity you'll *have* to religiously do, each month. It's the *only* way to stay on top of things, and ensure you're not backsliding into bad habits, losing control. It'll take some effort the first few times, but then, become streamlined and automatic.

Date	Item	Amount	Area
25/01/24	Savings	2,000	Save
01/01/24	Rent	18,000	Need
05/01/24	Car EMI	6,000	Need
02/01/24	Food	6,000	Need
10/01/24	Bills	2,000	Need
03/01/24	Maid	6,000	Need
10/01/24	Credit Cards	6,000	Want
10/01/24	Travel	2,000	Want
15/01/24	Entertainment	2,000	Want
	TOTAL	**50,000**	

Budget, sorted Area-wise

• • •

Tips for getting this done easily -

1. **Keep it simple.** Do *not* make huge long complex lists at the start, don't try to capture each and every rupee.
2. **Have a handle onwhere all the info is coming from.** Are your bank accounts, credit cards, bills, etc. available online, their apps enabled on your phone? Do you have payment reminders set up? As you get those alerts, keep adding them to your tracker sheet.
3. **Fix a date and time**, close as possible to salary credit, when you will review this. Check if anything is missing, needs to be added or modified.
4. **Don't lose this tracker.** Don't make it on the back of a diary or book used for other things, some random sheet of paper, or a file saved on your home computer. I personally prefer Google sheets - accessible, autosaving, available from multiple devices.
5. Once your salary hits, start making the payments - **and mark them off.** This way you know what's done, what's due, how much and when.

6. This won't make money magically appear; if you've overspent, you'll still have to pay, from savings or by borrowing. Any such adjustments will make their impact felt in the next cycle.

- Subtract the total expenses recorded from income received.

  - If there's a *positive* difference - expenses less than income - then, congratulations! You're already doing a good job, meeting expenses, and you have money left over. Add this into your 'Save' group.
  In the example above, the Save component is only 4% of expenses, which is very low. The goal should be to get it to at least 20%, i.e. 10,000.
  - If it's *negative*, spending more than you earn, don't panic - we've found the problem. We just need to fix it.

    - **Start cutting / reducing, starting with the 'Want' list.** Keep going until life looks just about bearable - nobody's asking you to eat *chana* daily and stay home your whole life. But, this point is where you have the first, and best, chance to get control of your budget battle. As long as that difference (income minus total expenses) is negative, you're losing. Is that new phone worth it? Why that expensive holiday, right now?
    - Once done, if the difference is still negative, and there's nothing left to cut... *then you have a major problem.* **Your lifestyle is unsustainable,** and sooner or later, it will ruin you. You're going to lose the war - it's time for *drastic* measures.

But before we do those (*because once you press that button there's no easy rollback*), check if the *other* number, the *income*, can be changed, increased.

Can you get a raise, a new job that pays you more, enough to cover the difference? Can you add any other regular, sustained income?

(*This is the final 'diplomacy' attempt before you go all out to save yourself.*)

Put a deadline on this - one month, six months, a year - whatever is sustainable - *but write it down*, in a visible place, and *stick to that date*. Every extra month you stay in this situation, your negative number - this is your increasing debt - is only going to keep getting bigger.

Didn't get that job? Then, it's time for **the last resort.**

• • •

To Do

If you've read this chapter, you already know what to do.

Make your budget tracker.

But I'm going to give you a little more work to figure out, and get you used to working on this.

- The 1ˢᵗ sheet is a basic tracker, which lists all the items, datewise. This is a data sheet only; every month, you have to add to this.
- One the 1ˢᵗ of the month, **enter all the planned or expected values for that month.** This makes the tracker a checklist of what is due to be paid and when.
- As and when you make those payments, **mark them off** by highlighting, or add & update a 'status' column.
- **Add other columns** as per your need - the date of payment, the account you paid from, the category (*like utility, travel, education, salaries, etc.*) and any others.
- Select the entire sheet, and **play around with creating pivot tables**. Can you make a pivot to summarize spends by month, year, category? Chart spends against item or category?

  The point of this is twofold -

  - to **build up familiarity** with the pattern of your cash flow
  - To get you **used to working with excel**, pivots, and charts, because they can be a powerful data-processing tool.

At the end of this, you should have a system where, for 2 hours per month of focused time, you can -

- track what comes in,
- track what goes out and when,
- make the payments,
- update the numbers,
- allocate the savings, and then
- **shut it and forget about it.**

• • •

CHAPTER XII

Reducing Needs

How can you reduce needs?

This is going to be hard to read, and it'll feel *very* overdramatic, scare-mongery, maybe a *little* ridiculous too. It's going to talk about doing something extreme, things that will make people around you think you've gone mad.

You'll scoff as you read, and imagine things will never get that bad.

They do. They get that bad, because they happen slowly, get worse and worse under the surface, and one day you wake up with your life screwed, and you have no idea how it happened.

Some people find a shortcut solution too - many times. Sell some stuff, jewelry, property, shares. Borrow. Cancel a couple of big spends. Push hard for a sales target. Clock some overtime. It *seems* to work.

But somehow, the problem keeps coming back.

It's a life-or-death situation. Your lifestyle's killing you, slowly but surely, and everything you tried to get it under control has failed - **and now, you're out of time.**

If you stay in this situation, then forget about managing your investments and growing money - you're sinking into debt, and soon, you'll be drowning in it. You need to get out, fast.

The trap that most people fall into is this - *they cannot believe that their situation is so bad, that they need to make these kind of decisions.*

They think they *still have time*, time to fix it, turn things around, make small adjustments here and there, cut this or that... but fundamentally, not making a huge paradigm shift. They think that the next raise, the next job shift will fix it, and it's right around the corner.

It isn't.

A negative cash flow is *not* a steady state of being; inflation is eating you, expenses are rising, lifestyle is by default going up. You're sliding down, and sliding faster and faster. Every day you stay in this situation, *makes it X times harder to recover.* You could spend the next 5 years correcting, fighting, slowly pulling the crashing plane of your life out of its death dive, maybe level off, assuming you don't hit a mountain along the way. But that's five years gone, and not coming back. You simply *don't* have the time for the easy way -the *hard* way is the *only* thing left.

Don't get me wrong - the easy way's still available, and most, almost everyone, takes it. They recover. They cut more expenses, use their bonuses, get a raise, get back on an even track. They think they're doing everything right.

But decades later, they look around, and wonder why *they* don't have a 4-bedroom house and a beach holiday home, 2 luxury cars, and no loans for their kids' MBA.

Compounding. Small changes made early add up to big differences later.

But a stable state gives you zero net positive, zero surplus to invest to compound up. And zero compounded is still zero.

• • •

The hard way

Some examples of decisions you now *need* to make in the hard way:
If not *specifically* these, then others, but at the same level. But this'll give you an idea of the *scale* at which you need to change.

- *Should you sell that house, if you can't afford the EMIs and maintenance?*
- *Maybe put it on rent instead, and move into a cheaper smaller rented house, further away? Move back with your parents?*
- *If your rent is too high, can you move to a cheaper locality, even if your friends are not around and you have to travel an extra 30-45 minutes?*
- *Can you sell that luxury car, and get a basic compact that still gets you from A to B? Or take the train?*
- *Do you need all the servants, driver, trainers, gym or club membership?*
- *Do your kids have to go to that specific school?*

See? These will be *very* big decisions, very *hard* decisions, and you'll feel *miserable* making them. You'll feel like a failure in life, like you've let yourself, and many others, down.

Maybe you'll slide into a dark depression, and find it hard to get out.

There *will* be arguments, fights, shame, guilt, questioning of life choices, a strained marriage, crying children, pitying looks from neighbors, mockery, and burning envy in your heart.

Expect this. Be ready for it.

It's OK. It's part of the process.

Bad as it gets, it's *still better than doing nothing* - because doing nothing is not just delaying the inevitable bad times, it's making the bad times way *worse,* and much harder to beat later.

The most important thing you *have* to remember, is this - what you are now doing is *atonement.*

You were greedy, ignorant, and you made some *bad* life choices. Now it's time to *pay* for them.

And one day, you *will* finish paying for them, and come out of the darkness, into the light again.

This is temporary.

You will have all this and more, once again.

Remember that goal, that light at the end of this dark tunnel. That light will *drive* you to get that better job, be more disciplined, and to keep that iron control over your money - and your life.

One day you'll come out, look back at the darkness, and know - that darkness past, *it's your friend now.* The memory of those bad times will *keep* you moving forward, knowing that you will *never* allow yourself to fall back there again, as long as you can fight it.

You have the time to do this today. Accept the pain, because you have the strength to bear it, today.

Wait till tomorrow, it might become too much.

Tomorrow, you might die in the dark.

• • •

CHAPTER XIII

Understanding Your Salary

So, you have job (lucky!) and get salary.
But CTC is not what comes in account. How to fix?
Go to HR dept. Ask what to do to get most in-hand. They will definitely have some solution (if you keep asking and sit on their head and refuse to give up).
They will say all nonsense about tax saving etc, but that you ignore.
Tell me, are you CA or lawyer? Have you done accounting? Did you even pass BCom?
Then how you will know all tax saving, NPS, EPF, 80C, etc? No, na?
So why do that? Just take all money you can get, and go!

• • •

One other thing to do, before we get into money management, is to figure out how *much* money we get.

The source - i.e. the monthly salary - is a very misunderstood place. Your salary structure may be running on default settings, and you're accidentally overpaying tax, misunderstanding cash flow, or under-utilizing useful features. It's worth it to take the time, and understand this, in some detail.

A salary structure for an employee (in most companies) can be defined in 5 components -

1. **Total CTC** - the max possible the company can spend on you (including salary, but also other things like benefits, contributions, bonuses, and covers tax as well)
2. **Gross Salary** - includes basic salary, plus stuff like overtime, bonuses, commissions, profit shares, and variable incentives, that may or may not be paid depending on performance; and reimbursements, that get paid out basis activity done, or performance (sometimes with some upper limit). Note, this also includes what will get cut in taxes, but excludes direct contributions like employer match to retirement
3. **Tax** - everything that gets cut. Income tax, professional tax, mandatory contributions, etc.
4. **Net Salary** - also called 'in-hand' - what you get, after removing the taxes (which the company usually cuts from salary and pays the government

directly), contributions towards retirement, etc. This is typically the monthly payment into the bank account.

5. **Benefits** - which may not be explicitly mentioned in a salary, but can be very important - health insurance, paid leave, maternity benefits, shuttles, car rental, free lunch, facilities, ESOPs, etc.

So, what you get, comes in 5 parts, in this order -

1. Opportunity to save for retirement (*before tax*) - This is something you get to enjoy much later, not today.
2. Taxes paid to the government (*you never get this back, maybe apart from some refunds*)
3. In-hand - what you actually *get* each month
4. Perks - Usually intangible to you, but with a clear cost component to the ompany (that's how it's added to your CTC). This can include things like free food, parking, paid leave, education support or free courses, commuting support, memberships, medical insurance, etc.
5. Variable or Bonus - What you get over and above the in-hand, sometimes, based on some variable factors. Usually annual, maybe quarterly of half-yearly in some cases.

Since the salary is the engine, the driving force of your cash flow, take the time to understand this well. It'll be very useful when you optimize it, or while you're evaluating an offer for a new job, or when asking for a raise.

One of the ways you can increase in-hand salary is by converting benefits and deductions to cash. For example, you can reduce your EPF or NPS contributions and opt to get that in cash. (*Bad idea! Not recommended - I'll explain below*)

To illustrate, let's consider a scenario where you have an option to opt for zero vs 10% contribution from your salary of 15,00,000 to EPF.

With EPF

Annual Salary	₹	15,00,000
EPF Contribution		10%
EPF Contributed	₹	1,50,000
Taxable Income	₹	13,50,000
Tax Slab		10%
Taxes	₹	1,35,000
In-Hand	₹	12,15,000

Without EPF

Annual Salary	₹	15,00,000
Tax Slab		10%
Taxes	₹	1,50,000
In-Hand	₹	13,50,000
Future Savings		0
Post-tax saving	₹	1,50,000
In-Hand Remaining	₹	12,00,000

Comparing Pre- and Post-Tax Savings

Without EPF, you just pay the tax and get an in-hand income of Rs. 13.5 lakhs. *Nice!*

With EPF, you pay 10% as EPF, then pay tax on the remaining 13.5 lakhs, getting an in-hand of just Rs. 12.15 lakhs. *Meh.*

BUT -

In the 1st case, you have 0 savings for future retirement. You get worried and put it in an FD or mutual fund or something. Now you have in-hand left over of Rs. 12 lakhs. *Boo-hoo!*

In both cases, you saved the *same* amount for the future, but ended up with *different* amounts in-hand, because of *when* you saved. That's the logic of EPF contribution benefits, and all other tax-saver instruments.

These benefits are supposed to incentivize retirement saving, so they *have* tax benefits (*i.e. they are 'paid out' before taxes*) - if you instead take that amount in hand, then income tax will also apply on them. If you take it all in cash, and then put that cash right back into some similar savings schemes (*like an FD*), then you're wasting a big chunk of it in taxes, without getting the tax saver benefits.

Why unnecessarily pay the government more tax, doing exactly the same thing - i.e. saving for the future? If you plan on using that extra cash to save for retirement, then it's better to save it *pre-tax.*

So, *when* is this justified? Only if you *need the cash for real emergencies*, or critical medical needs. Forgoing retirement savings *temporarily* to sort these is fine - but your goal should be to *get out of that situation, ASAP*, because you're living paycheck-to-paycheck and saving nothing. *Not* a good place to be in.

Clear that payment, then readjust the salary structure.

Another scenario - If you have a *very* high-interest loan, (*where you're paying a higher percentage in interest and charges than the tax rate + EPF return rate*) then it's better to forget the low-interest saving for now, and clear that debt first.

• • •

Save Tax by not being an employee

We'll go into some detail over how you can reduce taxes paid as a regular employee, but sometimes, it makes sense *not to be an employee at all.*

You can reduce your taxes paid by working as a contract employee, freelancer, or consultant. Here, you're paying your own taxes as standard 18% GST, and not the standard income tax (*as per salary slabs.*)

This can be financially useful in *higher* salary ranges, but you *do* lose out on some benefits offered only to employees. Check if losing those benefits is worth it - for example, do you already have private health insurance? Is the company likely to offer substantial payouts in terms of company performance linked bonuses or eSOPs, which only full time employees are eligible for? What about vacations, maternity leave, etc? At a career level, does this limit your long-term career growth?

One other thing to remember - as an on-roll employee, you get the benefit of association with a known company's brand, the '**Halo effect**' of that organization. If working at a highly reputed firm, this can help get you better loan rates, networking opportunities, social respect, visa approvals, conference invites, etc. This can add up over the years, and come in very handy when you need it the most. A consultant invoices the organization and gets paid, but doesn't get a salary slip. This can be a major problem when, say, applying for loans; you may not get preferential rates, or even be deemed ineligible, without that proof of employment.

Some things may be worth more than just money.

• • •

To Do

Get your salary documentation together, and set up a fixed place where you save / store these.

- Get your appointment letter (which should contain the salary breakup), the last Form-16, and the last couple of months salary slips. (You should anyway be saving these as a habit as soon as you receive them). Go through these, understand what is fixed, what is variable.

  - For the variable, list out what are the components / dependencies - i.e. what affects how much gets paid.

    - Your performance? Company performance? Something else?
    - Is there a multiplier?
    - What is the frequency this gets paid, and when?

- Check what tax bracket you fall into.
- See how much is being paid out in taxes, under what regime.
- Have a chat with your HR or Payroll guy, get his inputs on what can be adjusted / modified and what's frozen.
- List what you can claim for, and when. Do any of those come with an expiry date? When is that date?
- Are you contributing towards EPF or similar? How much? Is there an employer match?
- List out what you are paying out (*if anything*) in tax savers - life insurance, health insurance, PPF contributions, education loan payments, medical bills, rent, school fees, any tax-saving investments.

  - Specifically list what is the max amount allowed for tax saving in each category (80CC, 80D, etc,) and where you are against it today with your current contributions. (*Refer the worksheet for this*)
  - Set a goal for how much these contributions have to increase / reduce so you meet the criteria without dramatically falling over, or under, them.

- Do you have your UAN number, GST number, etc?
- Get your credentials set up for the government income tax filing portal.

Last - Find a CA. Take the docs to him, get his inputs on how the structure is, what can be done to (legally) minimize taxes.

The reason the *last* step is going to a professional, is because you need to have a basic understanding of your own situation. Then, you can objectively understand his recommendations.

It's ok if you aren't doing this - that's why we're here. As we move forward, we'll start building these. But first, it's important to understand what the starting point is.

• • •

CHAPTER XIV

Employer Benefits

After this, we'll get to starting payments; but first, a crucial checkpoint. One where you *claw back some extra cash.*

This will need a little research time, and contacts in HR and Payroll at work - try to block a day when there's little work going on, or many people in your day-to-day work are on leave.

Check out the company EPF (or equivalent), if there's an *employer match* - i.e. your employer adds X amount for every Y rupee you invest. Sometimes it's zero (*all saving responsibility is on you alone*), but *sometimes* there's a percentage match, which can even go up to 100%, depending on the organization policies.

If it's available, max it out. It's literally free money.

Plus, it reduces what you have to put into retirement funds on your own later, freeing up more liquidity.

Check out your HR policies' details for **benefits.**

- Are there car leasing schemes, special allowances, medicals, eSOPs, etc. that you are eligible for?
- What's the process for LTA, reimbursements and claims?
- If there are options that are pre-tax (eg, car leasing) that can be a substantially cheaper option than leasing from the market yourself, or even buying outright - if it matches your needs at the time.

If applicable, make sure you're *keeping track* of what all can be claimed or utilized... and have your *paperwork* ready. Track the last dates, save your reimbursable bills and eligible tickets, store receipts, and record any work-related expenses you did out of your own pocket.

It's a little bit of admin work, but worth spending an hour or two each month to process it.

It won't be huge, but every little bit helps - and you'll be surprised at what can be covered. Even a free breakfast or subsidized lunch can add up over time.

And, sometimes you'll find some silly mistakes - if you have a sign-in system, linked to attendance, make sure you show up on time, and don't get marked as accidentally absent or on leave. I've myself forgotten to swipe in many times, and unknowingly lost leave days for it. And if your company allows you to cash out leaves, that's a straight-up cash worth getting.

Even if not, who doesn't want a couple of random paid leaves occasionally to decompress? Mental health is important too.

• • •

ESOPs

For someone in early stages of their career, a big advantage of going to work in a startup or a smaller, newer, unlisted company, is the chance to earn ESOPs, Employee Stock Ownership Plans.

How it works - the company grants you an X number of ESOPs (*either one-time, or regularly added*) usually linked to your role, level, and seniority in the organization. If the company goes public (*or gets bought out*), you get an opportunity to *exercise* these ESOP options for that company's shares... which you can then choose to hold, or sell in the stock market at market value.

These *could* be worthless (*say, if the company shuts down before going public, or performs spectacularly badly*) or low value (*if you quit too early, there may be a buyback or cashout offered at some notional minimal value*).

But if you're holding a decent amount, and the company succeeds enough to list successfully, *then this can be a life-changing amount of money.* If you continue to hold, and the company continues to do well, the value of these will increase with the rise in the company's share prices.

You also don't necessarily have to join an unlisted startup for this opportunity - some companies have stock grant options as part of a compensation package. However, this is unlikely in the early stages of a career, and tends to be skewed towards senior, C-Level management.

In ESOPs, there is

- A grant date (when you are *allocated* the eSOPs)
- A vesting period (a time when you *have* them, but cannot *sell* them)
- An exercise date (when you convert them into *shares*). After this, you can sell whenever you like.
- A face value (a low notional value the company assigns to ESOPs, used for calculating how many to give. Eg. instead of a Rs. 1000 bonus, you could be given 100 ESOP options of face value Rs. 10)

So if ESOPs are offered as part of the compensation, you *seriously* need to do your research, and understand exactly what the potential of these could be.

• • •

To Do

Go through your company's intranet or HR policy section to understand claimable items.

- List out all the things you can claim for.
- Understand the claim process - an online portal, a physical submission, etc. What forms are required, what proof is needed?
- When are claims required to be submitted? Set a recurring reminder on your calendar a week before that date, ideally on a day when you have some free time to dedicate.
- Fix a place to keep bills and proof of expenses - a folder or box in your office drawer, a dropbox location, etc. As and when you get anything, just keep dropping it here.

On each occasion this reminder comes up, process your claims. It'll be painful and confusing at first, you will make mistakes, and will have to go to Accounts to clarify claims, cancel items, update or replace bills. All the more reason not to do this last-minute.

The second time, you'll be faster, with less errors. The third time, an expert.

Then it'll become automatic.

• • •

CHAPTER XV

Intermission 2

"Vinay, just listen to me. I'm telling you as much as I can - you have to trust me. Don't do this."

Vinay leaned back in the chair, his nervousness giving way to a heady sense of pride. This was unbelievable - the CMO himself, personally, was asking him to withdraw his resignation!

Now they finally understood his importance, how much he was benefiting the company - and now that he was quitting, they were shitting bricks.

Vinay had joined the startup straight out of college, his carefree, extrovert personality fitting him well into a business-development profile that he'd excelled in for a year. Then the pinch of a relatively low salary started making itself felt... especially when he met up with his other college buddies who, despite perennially bitching about psycho bosses and crazy targets, seemed to be able to afford clearly more expensive phones, better daru, and fancier bikes than him. They partied at hotter places, dressed flashier, and ate better.

He'd half-listen, enviously taking in everything... and after every catchup, he'd beg for contacts, if there were any openings, any way to get what they seemed to be enjoying.

And last week, it finally happened - 2 quick rounds of interviews, a brief negotiation... and an offer letter in hand, offering almost double of what he took home today.

He'd walked - no, floated - into office, fired off his resignation letter, and sat back and relaxed. There'd been a great many rumors flying around, for a while - this buyout, that merger, seniors locked up in conference rooms with clients and who knows, at all hours.

He'd grown tired of waiting, forever waiting for the myth of promised payoffs and vague rewards, that never seemed to materialize. It was time to move on.

Now, he almost felt sorry for the man sitting across from him. He must be regretting not giving a better joining offer, or a better hike - but that's life, he mused. The average employees stay, while the good ones move on, on to bigger and better things.

It was a pity, but he knew he could do better - it was time to spread his wings and fly.

"Thank you for your kind words, sir," he said, keeping a straight face. "But I am convinced I will have better growth and career with this move, and they are paying much better too."

The CMO leaned back with a sigh. It had been a long and frustrating conversation, but he also realized now that there was no point keeping it going.

"I see you've made up your mind to go, and I can't stop you - you've been a good person to have on the team, and I'm sure you'll do well in sales - but I just wish you'd think about this once. There's only so much I'm allowed to say right now - but just remember, your ESOPs get cashed out at face value if you quit now."

Vinay grinned inside. The ESOPs were worth practically nothing - he would cover that within a few months at his new job. "That's all right, sir," he smiled cheerfully. "I'm sure I'll be fine."

And then it was over; the handshake, the farewell party, the full & final settlement, which, when added to a cashed-out EPF, made a nice down payment for a brand-new bike, and he was off into his fabulous new career.

Six months later, the startup got acquired by a very well-known MNC. All his former colleagues got paid out an equivalent-value amount in the acquiring partner's equity.

Two of his ex-colleagues - less than thirty years old - literally retired. Three bought flats. Four got married. Five took year-long sabbaticals and went backpacking through Europe and Asia. Six went to do an exec MBA, while seven paid off their past MBA loans. Eight bought cars, nine set up own businesses, and ten partied harder for months on end, than he ever had his entire life.

And suddenly Mister number-one employee Vinay found himself right back where he'd started - on the outside, struggling, staring at someone else's glam life of luxury and plenty, except this was a life that he could have had all along...

...and missed out on.

• • •

CHAPTER XVI

BYOB: Be Your Own Boss

Should you be an Entrepreneur?

Being the founder of your own company sounds amazing - no boss, no rules, everyone looks up to you, anything can be a business expense, overnight success, and a tsunami of money flowing into your bank account.

But that's the 1% that's visible.

The other 99%, *it is the most terrifying, and the hardest, thing you'll ever do.*

True, you won't have a boss. You'll have *thousands* - every customer, client, investor, supplier, and team member.

You'll never have the luxury of saying, '*not my problem*' and walking away anymore. *Everything* will be specifically *your* problem to solve.

You'll never have a deadline. *Every single thing* that needs to be done, and isn't, can become a blockage that can gum up the eventual success of the whole. Every part of your business will be a quietly ticking time bomb.

You'll have to learn, and become expert, in every area, every big and small product and process your company uses and does. Not just the primary product - you'll need to know sales, finance, HR, logistics, marketing, admin, legal, IT, and hospitality, *and* know it well enough that you can't be fooled, can hire and evaluate people to do it for you, understand if they're doing it right, and step in and do it yourself in a crisis.

It's not one job - it's twenty plus. A hundred plus.

Both time and money will be limited, and therefore, anything else that takes them up is an opportunity cost. You'll never be able to think of spending money, or time, on *anything except your company*. No parties, cars, houses, vacations, hobbies. Your family will start to forget your face.

Your attack surface - places where you can be hurt - in a job, it's limited to what you're supposed to be in *charge* of. For example, If you're in sales, and the government passes a new law that stops you selling your product... then you can always shrug, pack up, and move to selling something else in a different company. It's not your problem to solve.

But as an *owner*, your life - and your business - is *over* if that happens.

And this can happen at *any* critical part of the entire structure.

Rewards do not come at month-end, or even year-end. They can take years, sometimes *decades*, to come. And all through this time, you've got to keep pushing with the same energy and belief, with no break, no backup.

One day you'll make it. It will all have been worth it then.

Maybe not for *you*. But hey, at least your kids' lives are sorted, right?

That's right - after going through all that, *you may not even get the chance to enjoy the rewards.*

So... nobody should be an entrepreneur, right?

It just sounds utterly miserable, and ultimately pointless.

No. The idea is more than an abstract thought, it's the dream that gives you a reason to get up every morning. If you've got *this*, then you'll never be able to imagine doing anything else. You'll never be able to think of giving up on it.

And you'll know you're the *only* one who can make it a reality - *nobody* else can be trusted to.

If you have this... then go for it.

But remember, you'll need at least *one of these two things*, over and above that.

1. **Experience.** It's much harder to be your own boss, because you have nothing to compare to, or any idea what to do. Even a *few* years' work ex, will give you a sense of how business works, how companies operate, and potentially, a network of contacts and clients that can be the backbone of the early years. Experience also tells you, if that idea, burning in your head - is it even workable, or realistic, or if anyone apart from you would ever want it.

2. Failing that, **an existing business** you are supposed to take over (*like a family business*) complete with an experienced, pre-existing mentor(s) who can, and will, teach you *everything* you need to know. This can still fail too, but it will have some people, systems and processes in place to buffer the collapse, and give you a chance to recover and course-correct.

Without one of these two, success is *exponentially* harder, time and money more easily lost in minor issues. Without these, even the mental capacity and discipline required, can be much harder to come by... because you never had the chance to develop and strengthen them in a wwork environment.

So, if you want to be an entrepreneur -

Don't do it for the glam.
Don't do it for the money.
Don't do it for the fame.
Don't do it for what you think it will make of you.
Just do it... for *it*.

• • •

Recap: Your Personal Finance Journey Checklist

Let's see how we're progressing through the journey, shall we? How many more of the list have we been able to check off so far?

I have -

- Decided to take control of my personal finances
- Allocated a dedicated storage area for my documentation
- Understood the basic concepts of inflation, compounding, and risk
- Made a monthly budget, and follow it
- Familiarized myself with my salary structure and all benefits
- Purchased life insurance with payout of at least a year's earning
- Purchased personal health insurance with all critical riders
- Set up an emergency fund of at least 3 months' income
- Automated standard bill payments
- Cleared all my outstanding credit card and high-interest debts
- Reduced regular debts to under 30% of income
- Started contributing to a functional retirement account
- Utilized fully the tax saver components of my salary
- Deployed goal-based RDs
- Saved in at least one long-term FD
- Created a diversified mutual fund portfolio
- Invested in a diversified equity portfolio
- Explored 1-2 alternative investments
- Secured my digital footprint and credentials
- Started researching alternative income streams
- Planned the regular biannual physical checkup
- Vacationed at least once a year
- Reviewed each of the above in detail every 5 years.

Expenses

We buy things we don't need, with money we don't have, to impress people we don't like.

Tyler Durden

CHAPTER XVIII

The Order of Priority in Payments

This budgeting is a pain, yaar. Do this, don't do that, do something later, do something now, too much. If I have to do everything, then let me do everything now. Too bad there is so much stuff, why you tell me make list and all? If no list, I can forget half, then enough money, no tension.

• • •

Right, here we are.

This is going to be the *most* critical part of the book, so - if you want to get a *chai*, take a little break, do that now. You'll need to *really* understand this, and remember it, because it will impact all money decisions coming up for the next 10-15 years.

Ready? Ok.

Some payments are more important than others.

You've got your budget sorted, and your salary optimized. It's time to start making payments.

Remember, about coming back to the 'Save' category? That saved money needs to get used, but it can't be randomly used anyhow, for anything - there's a specific order of things your cash, both regular and extra saved, has to power.

The order of payment is decided by how much of a difference each choice makes.

This comes from two things.

- A) What are the *chances* of this happening?
- B) What is the *impact* if it does?

A X B = the importance of any financial choice.

And so, we're back to **Risk versus Reward.**

Some events are very rare, but can have a *huge* impact, completely destroying or transforming the way life was supposed to go. Natural calamities like fire, flood, and earthquake that destroy everything. Killed in a car crash. Cancer.

The outcome lasts for decades, maybe the rest of your life.

Some are less rare (*in fact, quite likely to happen sooner or later*) but can have a major effect on life, savings, and plans. Losing a job. Moving. Business goes down, targets missed. Robbery, fraud. A broken leg while crossing the road at night, hit by a racing biker. Lockdown.
The outcome lasts for months.

There are also rare, but *good* things. Immigration, a new job in a different city. A rare opportunity to get property in a distress sale. Marriage, births. A 50% scholarship in a really good international MBA school. Inheritance. A lottery win.

And last, there's the inevitable. Expenses *will* increase. You'll age, get older. You'll stop working one day, your salary will stop. There will be other significant life events.

The whole reason we're doing financial planning is to have the ability to

-

- *First*, to negate or reduce harm, or risk of harm.
- *Second*, not to miss, or benefit better, from opportunities.
- *Third*, to become financially self-sufficient and independent.

These three things, and the sequence they follow, is the backbone of your *entire financial strategy*.
Safety, opportunity, and self-sufficiency.
Once you can take care of these, you'll see a fundamental mental change come over you - you'll not be worried for the future, free of indecision and confusion in your choices, immune to being tempted by greed or frightened by fear, and no longer a slave to a toxic workplace or people.

In fact, you won't *have* to do anything - you'll be free to do what you *want*.

• • •

So let's break up the above into specific items.
Safety

- Insurance
- Emergency Fund
- Debts and Loans

Opportunity

- Bills, Fees, Payments, Taxes
- Employer Benefits
- Tax Savers

Savings

- Bonuses and Windfalls
- Systematic planning for big spends

Self-sufficiency / Retirement

- Equities
- Alternate investments
- Parallel income
- Passive income
- Donations

That's it. That's your checklist for what needs to be handled, and when.

At this stage of your journey - in the first few years of earning - you should target *completely covering safety*, be ok to *experiment with opportunity*, and start to *plan for building self-sufficiency*. In that order.

As you cover each one, cross it off your list and ove to the next. Skipping a step messes with your ability to execute what you should be working on, and there'll be unease, a sense of danger hanging over your head.

Then over time, as your income grows, the amount of money and attention you're putting into each area will have to be checked. Not very often, but at least once in every few (2-5) years, is a good idea.

Another good time to re-evaluate, is shortly after you experience a significant life change (*ideally for the better, but bad events will also need to be evaluated, and your plan adjusted, accordingly.*)

With this approach, you're building a good, solid financial foundation to savings and planning, then slowly adding on top with opportunities to improve your savings, and finally building up the returns for future freedom.

At the same time, you're also building a strong *mental* framework that can allow you to know your position, assess your strengths and weaknesses, and evaluate every expense and opportunity calmly and rationally, aligned with how it fits in the overall scheme of your life and goals.

I assume by now you've done level zero - fixing your cash flow issues. You can't plan your savings in any meaningful way, if you *have* no savings.

These initial stages are boring, they only protect you from catastrophes. But they also give you room to experiment and grow later, and finally the last bit is the (fun!) long-shot plays, that can be life-changing.

• • •

To Do

Think about your existing spending, saving, and investing.

- Where does each thing it fit in the structure of the financial journey?
- All the potential opportunities, places to invest, ideas to make money - where do they fit?
- What are the risks if you neglect the sequence?
- Do some research, and then match the following:

Before Investing	• Mutual Funds • Gold coins • HUL and Reliance shares • Savings bank account • Bitcoin
Safety	• Public Provident Fund • A small 2BHK flat • New iPhone • Outstanding credit card bill • LIC term insurance • Collection agents
Opportunity	• Mother's eye operation • Rent • 2-week holiday in Europe • Shares in a hot new recently-listed smallcap firm • Additional income tax CA says I have to give • Petrol
Self-Sufficiency / Retirement	• ELSS tax saver fund • 5-year FD • Sandalwood farm deep the in Karnataka jungle • RD of 10% of salary every month • Food

Where does each item go?

• • •

CHAPTER XIX

Insurance

What is it?

Simply put, insurance is a financial instrument, where you '*buy protection*' by paying a small regular amount. This entitles you to get a large payout from the insurer in case of a specific (catastrophic) event, which you, on your own, would otherwise not be able to handle.

There's different types of insurance, specific to different catastrophes. We'll focus on 2 critical ones - Life, and Health.

• • •

Life Insurance

You pay the life insurance company Rs. X (a *premium*) every year, for Y years (the *term*) to a life insurance company. If you die, the insurance provider pays your family / dependents a Rs. Z amount (*coverage*).

You *don't* die, the insurance company *keeps* all the premiums. Since most people don't die (specifically as per defined conditions within the term period) the insurance company gets more money (total premiums) than what it spends (a few payouts), thus staying in business. That's basic term insurance.

(*There are other schemes of insurance where you get premiums back, or earn bonuses, etc, but these are just investment products with insurance attached, and have higher costs. I suggest to avoid them at this stage, and stick to basic coverage. That's what you actually need right now.*)

The chances of you dying tomorrow are low... *but not zero.*

Road accidents, earthquakes, tree collapse, a terrorist bomb, lightning, snakebite, road rage, faulty wiring... There are enough things, all around, that can kill you or anyone instantly, without warning. You don't even have to be in a dangerous situation (*extreme obesity, living in a war zone, hanging from trains, etc.*) for this to happen; never assume "*That happens to other people, not me*"

Obviously, the impact (of death) to *you* is infinite; nothing changes your life more than losing it. But there's also a devastating impact to your dependents, both current, and future. Even if you're not the sole or primary breadwinner for the family *today*, or don't have any dependents right now, that doesn't mean the same situation will always continue.

Which means, you need a life insurance policy that will give a payout equivalent to what those dependents will have lost, at least for enough time to let them find their feet. Figure out what that is, vs what premium you can afford today. Try and get at least a couple of years' worth of annual income, if possible, especially if you are the sole earner.

Do a basic term insurance, from a large, stable, reliable provider. Start as early as you can (*premiums are cheaper for younger and healthier folks*), and for as much as you can afford. (*The longer you wait, the older you get, the more expensive the premiums get*) The target should be to get coverage for at least a year or more of your annual income. As your income increases, so should (periodically) your insurance, either with new policies or additional top-ups.

Add riders to cover accidents and disability, and if applicable, preexisting conditions - those sometimes get forgotten, and any mistake or omission on your part is a perfect excuse for the insurance companies to deny settlement.

Remember, even if you don't die - but are sitting in a wheelchair, unable to work and earn - your income is gone, and at the same time your life insurance is useless at the moment. (*And if you stop paying premiums, will lapse - all your effort wasted!*)

Insurance companies are not inherently evil, out to screw you, but they *are* businesses, and they *will* follow an approach that nets them the best profits. It's not personal, it's just business.

Your job is to make sure you don't hand that opportunity to keep your money, to them on a silver platter.

Don't mix your insurance coverage with investing, tax saving, company-provided coverage or credit card benefits. Insurance is for insuring only. Stick to that.

Take care of the documentation - that's crucial in successful claims. Policy documents, premium receipts, etc. in a dedicated file, in a safe place, that everyone knows. You're not going to be around to tell them where you hid it, if they ever really need it.

Remember due dates. Keep a note of how much coverage you have over the years - as your income increases, you'll need to keep adding on.

• • •

Health Insurance

What is it?

Like in life insurance, you pay a health insurance provider Rs. X (*premium*) every year for Y years (the *term*). Instead of dying, like in Life Insurance, this type applies to situations where you fall sick and need treatment, and the insurance company pays for the cost of the hospital, medicine, tests, and treatment, (*coverage*). If you don't get sick, the insurance company keeps all the premiums.

You see how it's the same logic as death, but applied to *illness and medical expenses*. Sure, maybe you're healthy as a horse today... but that's exactly why you need to get it *now*. No pre-existing conditions, long premium-paying life, and an easy pass on the health checks, means better eligibility and super low premiums, that you'll not be able to get later when you're older, and likely much higher-risk.

Remember to check details about **what diseases / treatments are covered**, where you can get treated, who is covered (*Recommended to take for whole family*). Check what happens if you're already sick, (*pre-existing conditions*) when taking insurance. Get a cashless option - it lets you get the treatment and not have to run around later chasing claims.

Don't assume that every single expense is covered. Policies will differ in what they cover, how much, the settlement process, the proofs required, the specific treatments and hospitals. Spend some time reading through this and understanding it.

Take a private health insurance. Your company *might* cover you while you're an employee, but if you need it at a time when not employed, it'll be more expensive and stressful running around to get a new insurance in an emergency. Plus, different companies have different policies - you don't want to get caught off-guard in an emergency situation where you find out that something or the other, that you needed, isn't covered.

In both life and health, the older and sicker you get, the more expensive the policies get, so it makes sense to **get them early** - ideally from a company that's likely to be around as long as you plan to be.

Do the research. Find out what are some ranges for expected expenses, in some possible illnesses. Talk to your grandparents and parents about family histories, find out who suffered from, or died of what, and when it happened. Those are the more likely scenarios. When you choose coverage, ensure those are included. The size of coverage desired should depend on what these are likely to cost. Don't assume that there will be only one case across everyone, at all times.

Don't lie about lifestyle choices. You save a little on the premiums, but risk having a really large claim rejected when you really need it, making the whole exercise and your dutiful premium payments useless. Remember, risk vs reward. Small chance of it happening, but if - when - it does, you don't want anything failing, stopping you from collecting what you paid for.

And most of all, **don't forget inflation.** If something costs 10L to treat today, it will cost 20-30L when you contract that condition and need that treatment, twenty years from now. If that's too expensive to take today, that's ok - but remember to revisit and upgrade the policies five or ten years later, when you have more disposable income.

● ● ●

To Do

- Check if all policies have documentation available.
- Collect all policy documents
- Confirm if nominees are correct, or if there is a chance they may murder you for the insurance. If yes, change nominee to less murderous option. If a nominee is dead, or an evil ex, change it.
- List out all policies taken -

  - Insurance company, type of policy, premium amount, frequency of payment, duration of policy, premium date, riders, nominee, and coverage amount
  - Check if coverage amount is at least > 1 year of in-hand salary, and 2-3 years if nobody else is earning.

- Take a soft copy scan of policy documents
- Lock up all policy documents in a safe, secure folder
- Share this list of policies, and location of receipts and policy documents, with 3 people - a spouse, a parent, and a trusted friend with instructions to share to the previous 2 if you die.
- Set recurring reminder in calendar, 1 month in advance of premium due, with premium due amount
- Set up online payment portal credentials
- Set up a fixed storage location for all premium receipts, and sort by name, policy number, and date paid
- Check and add premium due in each month's budget, if any fall in that month
- Review the process for submission of these premium proofs to your company for tax declaration, and the last date of premium payment proof submission at work
- List all policies that are paid after that date but before year end. Find out the process for claiming the benefit for these as well.

• • •

CHAPTER XX

Intermission 3

"Please, just buy it na," Harsha had said, reaching across the table to squeeze his hand. They'd just finished watching a nice movie, he remembered, to celebrate. He'd been promoted to manager from assistant manager, with a 10% salary hike. It should have been a good date except for the third invisible person on their table, who had been inevitably butting in every time he met up with her. Her twin brother Harish, who had been trying to sell him some kind of investment product for the last few weeks ever since they met, and seemed to have recruited his sister as a client finder.

"I don't know, yaar," he said, trying to avoid it again. "It's a lot of money, and I don't really get what it-"

"Why are you being like this? You just got a promotion! You're earning! He's just trying to earn too, this is all he has, and you know how this has been a bad year for him! He's not going to meet his targets again and his boss is really horrible! He's been so worried all the time and not eating properly, and-"

"Ok, just calm down... I'm just saying, I don't know how this works, if I had some time to-"

He knew he'd messed up immediately. She pushed his arm away, sat back and glared at him.

"What, so now you don't have time also? You have time for movies and parties and coffee but you can't take five minutes to read the links I send you? Or you think my brother is some kind of fraud, a scammer, selling some fake cheating scheme? Is that it? You think we're going to take your precious money and run off, all of us, and go live in luxury in Mauritius on your stupid 60k?"

She looked away now, blinking furiously.

"Fine, don't trust me. Keep your precious money. Waaaiter!" she waved. "And I'll pay for my damn coffee also, ok?!"

"Ok fine! I'll take it! Tell him!"

Her face lit up, the frown vanishing, and she pulled out her phone. They spent the day at the mall, had a great time, and in the evening Harish had come over with bunches of forms and stickers pointing at where he should sign, thanked him profusely, collected his check and left. That had been two years ago.

He always thought, somewhere, that was where it all started to break. The quarterly payments (not annual as he had assumed) ate all of his increased salary, and a fair bit of his savings. He started to cut back on other things, shopping less, canceling the bike and continuing with trains. He asked some more friends about the supposed investment. All looked dubious and wary.

Not a single one bought it.

Over two years, his checks kept getting cashed, and the value kept dropping. Harish would no longer take his calls at all, or pass him off on a helpline number. Each year end he would try to invest into something else, at least for tax saving, but there would be no money left.

But most of all, every time he looked at Harsha's face, he could only see that money, and all the things he hoped to make his life better, vanishing. Her chatter, which he once found charming, began to sound brain-dead and grating. He became more and more sullen, withdrawn, only exploding out in more and more frequent arguments. They broke up that same year.

That evening he had tried to cancel, get back whatever he had invested. He couldn't. Going through the fine print in growing horror, he now saw for the first time phrases he had brushed over at first - '...lock-in period', '...forfeit', '...penalties', '...subject to market risk', and 'does not guarantee...'.

He got very drunk that night.

For a few more months he had hoped for the best, keeping up the payments, hoping it would turn around. It didn't. But he's finally managed to complete the two-year period of payments.

Now he can choose to cancel, and get back half of the current value (maybe a little less than a quarter of what he put in).

Or, he can continue to invest for a little longer, another year or two, hope the market does well, and he can get back maybe half his money.

Not having a girlfriend anymore has ended up helping; at least he can buy some tax savers now.

In the meantime, he still takes the train to work. 'It's like getting a massage every day,' he says to himself, staring into a sweat-shiny mustache hovering half an inch from his eyes, it's owners' surprisingly high, protruding stomach squeezing his lungs while an unknown umbrella handle digs into his kidney and someone's laptop bag rests on his shoulder.

'Next March,' he thinks, 'I will cancel this, take whatever I get, and put it for the bike EMI.'

'Then maybe, one day, I will find Harish crossing the road in front of me. And then I can run him over.'

● ● ●

CHAPTER XXI

The Emergency Fund

So, now you're sorted for either dying, or serious illness. What *else* can go wrong, so badly, that all your plans fly out of the window?

You don't have to die, or go to hospital, to lose your ability to provide for your family - your employer can sometimes decide that on your behalf, i.e. downsizing.

Losing a job, getting fired or laid off, not getting work for a long time, delayed payments from clients, a poor period in business, or some random act-of-god catastrophe. All these mean your regular monthly salary drops steeply, or stops completely.

When that happens, even if it lasts a short period - if you don't have anything saved - you'll be forced to sell your car, furniture, and possessions, you'll begging your parents to sell their jewelry or ancestral property, and eating a single meal a day... and all the while, in *full panic mode* about where your next meal is coming from.

Forget about making any investments now, however good the opportunity is - you won't be able to even *think* straight.

This has a bigger impact than you think. You won't be able to give interviews properly when applying for jobs, you'll take bad advice, from the wrong people, not negotiate effectively in job offers for the role and pay you deserve, and end up setting your career back years.

In that panicked state, it's going to be *that much harder* to recover, and to get back on track.

But, what if you had someone to pay you during this bad time, while you look for a new job?

How *awesome* would that be? Imagine... chilling at home, no boss, no commuting, no meetings, no updates and reports... just you, in charge of your own time, focusing on researching and getting your career back on track. No worrying about bills, fees, EMIs, and food... at least for a little while.

Good news - there *is* a person who can pay you like this, for as long as you want. *You.*

An emergency fund is supposed to cover all your *'Needs'* amount, for as many months as you think you'll need, to recover and get that new job.

Example.

For a 3-month fund, if your salary is Rs. 20,000, and your monthly needs are Rs. 15,000.

Then you need an emergency fund of Rs. (15000X3) = Rs. 45,000.

If you want to take a year to save it up it, set a monthly RD for (45,000/12) = Rs. 3,750.

Do *not* spend this.

As your needs increase over time, your emergency fund has to keep pace - keep expanding it.

Sorry - during this emergency time, there'll be *no* savings, *no* random shopping, *no* leisure activity, *no* holidays.

This is important. Life can be difficult, but not unbearable. It'll keep you motivated.

"But," you ask, *"How will I know how long it will take to get a new job? You think I can see the future?"*

No - you can't see it, but *can* influence it. If you think you can get a job fast, keep a smaller amount. If you want to take time, put more. **3 months is minimum, 6 is good.** More is overkill - there are better ways to use that much cash, and having too much in reserve makes you lazy.

Calculate that number you need, and set it as a target - I will have this fund amount by so-and-so date - and then start putting aside cash every month towards it. Set up this as an RD, but make sure it stays unusable - don't accidentally spend it when it matures.

I will repeat - this money *cannot* be spent, unless a *specific, defined emergency situation* happens. A Diwali Amazon sale on a 72" TV, 30% off on flights to Phuket, those are *not* emergencies. Your best friend about to get beaten up by the bouncer because his credit card declined, that is *not* an emergency. A credit card bill with huge late fees is *not* an emergency. Spending for all this from an emergency also wrecks the effectiveness of your budget, making you feel you have more than you actually do.

You save until you hit your target amount, and you do *not* stop saving until then.

Once you hit it, convert it into an FD or similar - ready to be broken if needed.

- It cannot be left lying around as available cash, it *will* get spent, nor in a savings account (inflation will eat it up).
- It cannot be locked up in a hard-to-liquidate thing like property - you can't get it out fast without a loss-making distress sale.
- Don't put it in a risky place like stocks, where value will fluctuate as per the market. You can't convert it into gold coins and jewels, lock it in a box, and bury it under the big banyan tree haunted by the spirit of the old zamindar embodied in a giant cobra, in your remote ancestral village 2 days' drive away. It has to be reachable, accessible in 24 hours... but not in 5 minutes.

Keep it accessible, but not *too* accessible. Be clear on what it's going to be used for. Define those conditions, and then maintain the sanctity of those conditions.

Don't waste it on *anything* else. Once you start, you'll keep finding excuses to spend... and one day it will be all gone, and as per Murphy's Law, *that day will be the day before you lose your job.*

• • •

To Do

Set your emergency fund goal.

- Go back to your budget sheet, and list out the necessary items only (needs) for the last 3 months. Include 1/12 of mandatory annual payments like insurance and school fees.
- Average each item to get a per-monthly cost.
- Add it up, multiply by 3 (for 3 months of funds). Don't get stuck if you don't have an exact number - a rough estimate is fine.
- Add 10% safety margin.
- *This* is your minimum goal.

Write down a specific, stringent list of 5 situations which qualify as an emergency. Eg - Losing a job. Accident or medical emergency. Natural disaster. Fire in the home. *Only* these will qualify for accessing this fund. You'll know what's a real emergency, and what's just fooling yourself, as you write this.

If you have a spare bank account where you can accumulate this, use it, else open a new account. Activate the ATM card, set up netbanking, add your regular account as beneficiary, or that of your spouse or any other person who might need funds in an emergency. Lock it up in a drawer, along with the checkbook. Do *not* keep it accessible via phone apps or UPI. Do *not* take a credit card.

- Set up a monthly transfer (around 5th of the month) of an amount 1/12 of the minimum goal to be paid automatically into this. Do it for a year. If you cannot afford 1/12, make it 1/24 and do for 2 years. Paying this takes priority over any other wants.
- Alternately, you can also set up an RD in your emergency fund account of the amount you're putting in. This can give you a slightly better interest rate.
- (*Optional*) once you hit your goal, convert to FD (keeping up with inflation). We're doing this to make it a little harder to 'accidentally' spend this emergency fund.

After you have 3 months' funds, repeat the cycle, at a slower pace, to reach 6 months of funds.

Remember - in an emergency situation, only *needs* are to be met. This is not a retirement fund, nor a 'life as usual' situation. It's an *emergency*, which means all your attention has to be focused on getting out of the emergency, without worrying about rent and food.

• • •

CHAPTER XXII

Critical Needs – Bills, Fees, Payments

In your budget tracker, keep a sharp eye on fees, payments, and bills. There's two reasons to do this.

One, to know what you owe, track when to pay or renew, don't get fined for late fees.

Two, to have an idea of usage, and identify wastage - don't pay for something you don't use.

- **Step one, automate the critical basics.**

  - **Utility bills** - i.e. electricity, phone, internet, cable, gas, etc. These are billed monthly, and are generally not huge (unless you run a bad AC, 24/7).
    I recommend **setting up autopay** for these from your account, for less headache in tracking individual due dates.
  - Electricity - Heavier consumption comes from ACs, heaters, electric cookers, geysers. Opting for energy-efficient options in these first, or reducing usage, can make a significant difference.
  - Mobile - consider combining multiple users into a family plan, rather than individual plans. Check periodically for new plans / providers if a better deal is available.

- Next, your **optional subscriptions.**

  - Netflix, Prime, all the OTTs, music streaming services, online storage, digital services, paid apps, device protection plans, premium memberships, gaming accounts, physical and digital magazines and newspapers, etc... You'll be surprised how many come up, once you start listing them.
    Now, do you have a clear idea of what subscriptions you have, how much you're paying for them... and are you actually *using* them?
    Make a list, including fees. Typically these are set up to auto-bill from your credit card, right from registration, so it's easy to forget about them, and end up blindly keep on paying long after you stopped using

them. *Especially* dangerous are the free trials, that quietly slip into paid without warning.

- **What about your real-world subscriptions?**

  - A club or gym membership, school or extracurricular activities, kids' programs or tutions, society facilities charges, staff or house help salaries, appliance or car servicing, tech support. Some are big ones like school fees, annual society charges, tax filings, etc. Sometimes you don't know exactly what you are going to spend... but you can have a good idea of when, and approximately how much.
  - Even more troublesome are ones that don't happen on a regular monthly basis - those tend to accumulate in the background, then suddenly hit you with a big lump-sum payment. Don't get caught off-guard by these arriving unexpectedly, and throwing off plans.

List. Everything.
Put it in your budget tracker. Even if it's a zero amount 11 months out of 12, just add it, so you do remember it, when it *does* come due.
We should keep paying the necessary bills, by default, because -

- **One**, an interruption here, is a disruption in daily life's functioning.
It's a base level of keeping everything running; while paying loans and investing for the future is important, that works better if you do not have to wash dishes by candlelight, because you ran out of money to pay your *bijli ka bill* and the *bai*.
- **Two**, once it's laid out transparently in front of you, you can take a call on doing some optimizing. Do you really *need* all this? Are you overpaying for something that doesn't work, or you barely use? Are there redundant, overlapping services?
Can you put a date on when to terminate some, or at least start using them, and get your money's worth out?
Build a phasing-out plan for unused subscriptions.

I know - all this seems to be a *lot* of effort for something relatively minor. A few hundreds, at best thousands, here and there. But it's not about the *amount* at this point; it's about building *discipline*, creating good habits to retain control and awareness of what you're doing. Getting this ingrained into your mindset will let you track future investments and SIPs in exactly the same way... only this time it'll be counted in the tens and hundreds of thousands.

● ● ●

To Do

- List, then set up autopay for utilities via direct debit from account. Almost all banks support this.
- List, then review all your subscriptions.

  - Drop / Cancel what you don't use.
  - Set up auto-renew for the rest from a designated online-only card with a low limit. (*Digital safety - we'll talk in more detail about this later.*)

- Make a tracker - on another sheet in the budget file - listing, roughly, how much is being paid out on what day of the month.

  - Segregate the monthly, quarterly, and annual bills.
  - Add it up (within each type), and put it as a 'subscriptions' item in your budget.

• • •

CHAPTER XXIII

Working Abroad

If you get the chance, work outside India. For a bit.

The *experience* is priceless. The transition into a wholly new environment gives tremendous neural, psychological, and social benefits, apart from the expected boost to the career, and monetary perks. You get a chance to learn new fields, make new connections, build a network, and experience some very different people and ways of working.

However.

Make sure you do this for the *right reasons*. Going abroad just for the sake of going abroad, or because your friends are doing it... that's going to land you with very expensive problems, and possibly in dangerous situations, that can be very hard to get out of.

When you should go -

If you have a job offer from a known, reputed firm, in a relevant area for your career; an internal transfer within your own company for a better profile or experience; or an education opportunity, with admission from a good university, and relevant for the job market there.

What is 'known', 'good', and 'reputed'? You need to do your homework for this.

Agents?

I'd say, be cautious. They can help and guide you, but they're not *responsible* for you. They'll charge a fee, and follow their checklist. Whether you get through or not is irrelevant, so don't put all your trust and faith in them.

And if there is any mention of under-table dealings or less-than-legal activity, walk away. You're risking investing a *lot* of time, money and effort... only for a visa rejection at the end. Or even worse - a future fraud detection and deportation, meaning no trying, ever again.

And please do not do any *bullshit* shortcuts like going on a tourist visa, and then trying to find work. You *will* get caught, and a violation like that pretty much means the end of any aspirations you may have had for that country.

Research, research, research.

Keep in mind that moving to, and working, in a new country can also be surprisingly expensive in unexpected ways. Do your research, find out and set expectations, identify useful contacts, and have a plan in place before you go.

Research the process, the place, the opportunities, the culture, potential contacts, job scene, costs, laws, risks, future career paths, requirements, documentation, emergency plans, everything. Take the time to do it properly, because it will take a lot of time.

When you're there -

Don't go into the extreme case of sharing a tiny room in a bad neighborhood with 7 other people, all eating once a day, and desperately saving every penny to send home.

You're *there*, which means it's a *huge* opportunity to network, build contacts, and have experiences that can open future opportunities that could be worth a lot more than whatever you save today.

Don't squander that. *Live the life.*

But also, *stay grounded*; don't leap into a frantic hedonistic holiday mode, where you end up spending on unnecessary luxuries, or building an unsustainable, high-end lifestyle that gets you in trouble, leaves you with expensive vices, and blows up all your savings. It's easy to lose yourself in the change - having a plan will keep you anchored.

When returning -

No, don't run up bills before you leave and expect them to just forget it. Keep your lifestyle in control, you won't have huge debts - and small debts are always best left settled. Different countries have different laws, some harsher than others, and everything is networked. All it'll take, is one flight re-routing to a changed stopover, an auto alert to the airport police, and you'll be whisked off to jail the instant your wheels touch the ground.

• • •

CHAPTER XXIV

Recap: Your Personal Finance Journey Checklist

Let's see how we're progressing through the journey, shall we? How many more of the list have we been able to check off so far?

I have -

- Decided to take control of my personal finances
- Allocated a dedicated storage area for my documentation
- Understood the basic concepts of inflation, compounding, and risk
- Made a monthly budget, and follow it
- Familiarized myself with my salary structure and all benefits
- Purchased life insurance with payout of at least a year's earning
- Purchased personal health insurance with all critical riders
- Set up an emergency fund of at least 3 months' income
- Automated standard bill payments
- Cleared all my outstanding credit card and high-interest debts
- Reduced regular debts to under 30% of income
- Started contributing to a functional retirement account
- Utilized fully the tax saver components of my salary
- Deployed goal-based RDs
- Saved in at least one long-term FD
- Created a diversified mutual fund portfolio
- Invested in a diversified equity portfolio
- Explored 1-2 alternative investments
- Secured my digital footprint and credentials
- Started researching alternative income streams
- Planned the regular biannual physical checkup
- Vacationed at least once a year
- Reviewed each of the above in detail every 5 years.

Liabilities

If you cannot control your emotions, you cannot control your money.

Warren Buffet

CHAPTER XXV

Debts and Loans

Breathe.

If you got this far, you're in a good place.

Now, even if the worst happens - you have room to move, control over choices, and you can't be forced into bad decisions.

Now, let's get your cash-flow problems fixed.

High-Interest Debt

We talked before about credit card late fees. That's an example of high-interest debt - something with a *very strong negative impact* on savings, because it's continuously, heavily 'bleeding out' - a lot of money that keeps vanishing, with nothing in return.

Imagine filling and storing water in a bucket. High interest debt is like a large hole, right at the bottom, so water is leaking out hard & fast. You've got to keep running to refill it again and again, pouring in much more than you actually use... and if you stop refilling, all the water's soon gone.

Almost all loans - personal, auto, buy-now-pay-later schemes, 'easy' EMI - they all have something in common. *They are designed to take your money.* They dress it up in sheep's clothing of "convenience", "points", "freebies", "rewards", and "discounts", but under it, will always be the wolf of **fees.**

Credit cards, and these type of loans, carry some of the most *expensive* fees you'll ever have the misfortune to meet. Carefully hidden in the terms & conditions, they're not always common-sense logical, but deliberately designed traps to snap shut on the unwary, and catch them in a continuous, never-ending cycle of payments.

The payment structures, applicable fees, credit limits and interest rates - these are carefully engineered, by brilliant, genius-level minds and high-powered algorithms, to do *one* thing, and one thing *only - get the maximum amount of money out of you.*

How does this work?

When you buy something on your card, you're borrowing from the bank, with a promise to pay back by the due date. If you can do this, you're fine - nothing extra charged, convenient and easy.

Banks hate this.

What they *actually* want, is for you to spend so much, that you *can't* pay it all back. And *that's* where their fees kick in.

That's why your card doesn't stop working if you miss a due date; the pending amount rolls forward on the next payment cycle, with late fees and interest payments added.

These fees are how the banks make money. *That's* why they give high limits, offer minimum payments - they're giving you a chance to run up a high, unpayable bill. Then, when you try to pay it off, even by reducing your card usage - the fees, penalties and interest payments ensure the pending due amount reduces very slowly, maybe even *increases*.

Example.

Your bill is Rs. 100,000, and minimum payment is Rs. 1000.

You find you can't pay it all for whatever reason - so you do that minimum payment only.

Your next bill now has previous outstanding added to it, less minimum paid - i.e. 99,000 - and the interest charged. And that interest isn't going to be small, ranging from 18% to 24% or more.

This looks low superficially, but adds up. CC interest is typically compounded daily - so every day you don't pay, yesterday's interest is added to the total, on which the new interest is charged.

So even if you completely *stop* using the credit card, as long as you are making just minimum payments, your *total's* still getting bigger and bigger.

Credit Card Billing		
Interest APR %		18%
Month 1 bill	₹	1,00,000
Minimum paid	₹	1,000
Outstanding	₹	99,000
Interest charged	₹	1,485
Month 2 bill	₹	1,00,485
Minimum paid	₹	1,000
Outstanding	₹	99,485
Interest charged	₹	1,492
Month 3 bill	₹	1,00,977

A Credit Card Bill is Forever

You see? If you're stuck in a loop of part-payments, or minimum payments, you end up paying much *more* than whatever it was you used the card for, and paying for much *longer*, over and over.

And if you miss even the minimum, *additional* late fees and penalties are charged, each time... and your APR (interest payable) also goes up, and stays up, for months, making subsequent payments even more expensive.

Banks *love* this cycle - for them, it's a steady income stream. They also know that once someone's caught, it's in a spending habit that's hard to break - and they count on it. That's why they give points for spending on CC, lounge access, cashback, discounts.

They *want* you to spend, get *used* to spending, spend even more, and *keep on spending.*

If the credit card stops working, then you stop spending, are *forced* to break the habit. Embarrassing, but good for you in the long run.

Not for the bank, though. A canceled card means no more fees and payments, no more revenue stream. So, the banks offer you a conversion to EMI - this reduces your immediate bill, but creates regular future ones. This ensures you keep using the card, but also keep paying in the future.

• • •

By the way, those minimum payments you were making? You were only paying *interest!* You *still* have an unpaid loan against your name, meaning you're *still* going to keep being charged interest, and your credit score's gone for a toss.

Typically, an annual interest rate can come up to be around 18% to 24% - that's higher than almost every other place you borrow money from, except maybe the local *bhai* - who, at most, will break your legs if you don't pay up - but even he won't give you even *more* money, so he can later break your arms as well.

That high interest rate means, this problem has to be solved before *anything* else.

It won't make sense to save money in the bank (*4% interest*), or make an FD (*7%*), put in PPF (*8%*), invest in mutual funds (*likely 12%-15%*) or even blue-chip equities (*20% if you're lucky, never mind the risk*).

Any of these are still *worse* than paying off the loan, because the loan is taking money out of your pocket faster than you, and your investments, can put it in.

If you're bleeding heavily, don't start gulping down iron-rich food to replace blood - first put a bandage on.

• • •

The *other* side of the situation - where you pay nothing, just *stop* paying, completely, because you're ruined or have given up - that's *also* not a good outcome for the bank, because their revenue stream will stop.

They'll try their best to persuade you to continue. Offer EMI options, loans, attractive looking plans.

But once they realize this revenue source - *you* - is effectively dead to them, and cannot be used as a cash cow anymore, they take the last step of just handing it off to *collection agents.*

This has 2 outcomes.

- **One,** whatever the agent can squeeze out of you, is *still* a little more than what they could have got... so, it's a minor bonus. It's like working you to death... then selling your corpse to medical college for a few bucks.
- **Two,** they let the collection agents create such a *notoriously* negative experience, that others won't be tempted to give up and rebel like you.

It's a public hanging - the objective is not punishment for the one who was caught, but *deterrence* for the ones that weren't. They want the rest of people caught in payment cycles to look at what happened, and *shiver* in fear of the same happening to them. Insults, humiliation, public shaming, emotional trauma, threats & intimidation, and casual, indiscriminate violence. They *want* those other poor people peering from their balconies and their social networks to see... so that they, when it's their turn, do *whatever* they can to avoid the same fate.

*I'm sure there'll be plenty of backlash at this. I'm not accusing any specific person or institution, of following any specific practice. But you **know** this happens... just follow the logic. Any organization is incentivized to earn profits, and is going to naturally favor methods, that enable those profits.*

Yes, there are ethical players in many industries that restrain themselves and partners - but you and they are not friends and family. You are a revenue source to them, and they are in business to earn revenue.

They don't owe you kindness, understanding, or consideration.

They owe you nothing.

Microfinance, Auto, and Personal Loans also fall in this high-interest debt category. Even that zero-interest EMIs X 6 months, build in charges - *nothing is ever free*, and everything is usually much more expensive than you thought. And unlike home or education loans, these can't even be adjusted against tax benefits.

• • •

TL;DR version -

- Keep a tight control on credit card spending and bills.
- Pay off all outstanding debt as quickly as possible.
- Cut back spending if the debt's getting out of control. (*The first missed payment is the sign that it's already out of control.*)
- Don't be fooled by Marketing and PR, and the promise of convenience and ease.

• • •

To Do
This is a two-step process.
First - what are your outstandings?

- Make a list of all your credit cards, including the bank, the due date, the amount.
- Add a 'purpose' against each - is this meant for shopping? Groceries? Restaurants? Petrol? Flight tickets? Online payments? This is useful if you have multiple cards, to avoid spending indiscriminately on all of them. If you have just one, then it doesn't matter. Label the cards to help you remember.
- Ideally, you should have two -

  - A. a low-limit one for occasional online orders and subscriptions, as these are stored online and more susceptible to getting hacked or stolen.
    (I leave it to you to decide what is 'low' as per your usage ;))
  - B. a higher limit one to use at PoS machines at retail outlets and restaurants.

You can use a tracker app to get reminders and see the analysis - do your research to make sure it's safe first. Otherwise, use the good old excel sheet.
The **second** step... comes after the *next* chapter.

• • •

CHAPTER XXVI

Escaping the Debt Trap

Help, get me out of here!

So all that's great, but what do you do if you're *already* caught in a debt trap?

Imagine this situation. You overindulged, and now, you have a CC bill too big to pay off, bigger than your monthly salary.

What can you do?

I'm sorry... you don't have too many options here.

First, look at your budget. Pay your insurance premiums, the critical bills, the rent and the EMIs. Keep putting money for the emergency fund. Take care of the basics before anything else.

Then -

- **Option 1 -**
  Sit quietly and live the simple *sanyasi* life until you have finished paying that bill, part payment by part payment.

No shopping, no eating out, no travel, *no nothing.* As long as that full bill remains unpaid, you're losing money at a rate that *can't* be sustained in normal life. Therefore, life needs to be *abnormal,* until this ends. If there are some very large expenses on that bill, call the bank and have them converted to EMI. It prolongs the process, but reduces the intensity to a manageable level.

Imagine this. Your finances have had a bad accident, lying wounded by the road, blood gushing out everywhere. In this state, you don't go to work, attend meetings, go for a movie. You go to the hospital and lie very, *very* quietly until you've been fixed up, until the bleeding's stopped.

A second positive outcome of this is, it's a *money detox* - an opportunity to break free of some expensive habits, you may not realize you never actually needed.

- **Option 2 -**
  Counterintuitively, another solution is even *more* loans - called *debt consolidation.*

Instead of having a series of different loans, credit cards, wallets, etc, where you can't keep track of what has to be paid when, different fees, multiple people following up, just add them up - *and get a single large loan to pay them all off.*

Then, gradually, pay off that one single large loan, keeping a tight control over the date of payment and tenure, all the while ensuring the earlier situation doesn't come back on your other activities.

Obviously, you can't do this often - and once you do it, you can't repeat it again next month. Do not let those individual cards run up again.

Break the habit. No point taking and paying the loan, but also running up more bills at the same time, creating the need for another loan.

• • •

Now, let's think of an even *worse* scenario.

Let's say, you *do* find this happening again, and again.

What are you doing wrong?

Step back a moment. *There's a deeper issue here.*

You haven't solved the *original* problem that put you here - you're simply spending too much.

Like a yo-yo diet, going on a spending spree to somehow make up for months of denial while you were paying off the first bill or loan, will leave you worse off than before - back in debt, right back where you started, *and* mentally fucked in the bargain.

At this point, you have no choice.

• • •

Cancel the credit cards - which means actually call the bank and cancel. Don't just cut and throw the physical card, but leave saved accounts on the ecommerce sites and QSR apps.

Go back to UPI, debit or physical cash. When your balance runs out, you simply have to... stop. There's no risk of spending more than you can afford.

And as you watch the 500s notes get replaced by 100s, and the 100s replaced by 20s, you'll automatically scale back from Starbucks to the downstairs tapri. After a while, it'll become a habit. And you can still enjoy that mochachino - just not on a daily basis.

Trust me, doing this - it will be *hard*.

You'll run into situations where you have to take out items from your basket in the checkout queue. Back out of parties and holidays. Miss out on sales, events, experiences.

You *will* feel poor. It'll be embarrassing, humiliating. It'll cut you off from your friends and peers. You'll be called boring, no fun, miserly, *chindi*. You'll be left out of plans and parties.

It can possibly drive you into depression.

That's the price of healing. Are you ready for it?

• • •

Try to understand the *habits* that got you here.

- Do you have a bunch of different cards, and lose track of when to pay what?
- Are there some automatic subscriptions, set for things you don't need?
- Do you daily pass by a place that prompts or tempts you to spend?
- Do you have a widespread friend circle or office groups, meaning there's always someone asking you to eat / drink / party out several times a week?
- Are you doing online shopping by default when bored?

Maybe... *these* are the things you should start avoiding.

• • •

Last - look hard at your *motivations* for spending.

Why do you feel like spending?

Is there some frustrated desire that you aren't able to make happen - so you're channeling that into owning things? Some sense of missing a part of life that you're subconsciously compensating for?

Are you trying to buy happiness?

Because no credit card in the world, has a high enough limit for *that*.

• • •

To Do

Look at the tracker sheet for credit cards you made.

- Add up the outstandings.
- Check what the (annual) interest rate is being charged.
- *Can you clear these outstandings each month?*
- Or are you rolling over, making minimal payments, racking up late fees, interest payments, and incurring penalties?

If you are struggling with the second one, then -

- Get a cheap (low-interest) loan, from a reputable loan provider - co-op banks, government banks, or, best option, your own family - embarrassing, but a very good option in payment terms, with built-in benefit of constant supervision.
- Pay off everything on all the credit cards.
- Cancel all but 2 critical (best) credit cards.
- Do not keep spending on the credit cards.
- Pay off the loan. (*This payment should now be in your monthly budget 'needs' category.*)

Next - Understand your usage.

This is an optional step, but can be a very useful thing to do as a one-time activity if you want to understand what's happening. Also very tedious, so do it only if you're really curious.

- **Download** the last 6 months of credit card bills, preferably as excel.
- **Copy-paste** into one place, adding columns to identify which card, and dates.
- **Clean up** the data, converting text to numbers and dates, removing junk, fixing the format. Test this with an AI.
- **Replace** purchase codes with store names. (Some googling will be needed here)
- **Add** broad *categories* against the stores - clothes / electronics / restaurants / events / etc
- Run a **pivot** to see what *categories* are responsible for max spending.
- Finally, consciously **reduce** in the highest ones, as much as you can. Zero may not be possible, but 50% can be done.

Why do we do this?

Doing this will change the credit card bill, in your mind, from a scary, unknowable, black-box demand for payments, to an understandable *story* of your *habits*. It will reveal something about you, a weakness, a soft spot. It will show you to be a person who cannot resist A, B, and C - so the *next* time an A, B, or C comes along, you'll *recognize* them as something to be especially wary of.

If you want to get control of your credit card spending, you then need to *control* these habits.

And while controlling habits is a whole other subject, with completely different sets of books, coaches, and the works, but think about this - *why do you have these habits?*

What are you trying to achieve, or solve, or prove?

It's a big question - but you've taken the first step, of breaking it down into smaller parts, so you can understand and systematically fix each one by one.

Think about it, calmly and rationally. It sometimes helps to write things down.

• • •

CHAPTER XXVII

Regular Debt

All *right*, we're making progress!

You've taken care of emergencies, and you've stopped money flowing down the drain.

Now, look at everything else that's taking your money out of your pocket. Anything you *owe*, all the other loans - Car EMIs, payment schemes, personal or education loans - all these are slowly sucking away your money. They may not charge you credit card rates, hopefully, but they are charging *something*, which means a net-negative flow.

Your priority needs to be getting these to zero.

Also, as long as there's any loan being repaid, there's a risk of missed payments - meaning penalties, fees, and overall less room to maneuver.

No new suggestions here, apart from the basic one - if you owe something, paying that back quickly, and safely, has to be a priority.

Quickly, because you want to get to a place as soon as possible where you can invest and grow your money. Compounding needs time.

Safely, because you still have to ensure the basics of planned expenses and emergencies need to be in place. No point paying loan A, realizing you forgot to factor in your wife's birthday, your kid's term fees, and a tree falling on your car, and running to get loan B.

The less outflow you have, the better you can use the inflow; use it to invest, and get yourself returns, instead of sponsoring finance companies.

Keep in mind - paying off these debts can - and should - still happen alongside *other* investing. I understand it may not be possible to live completely debt-free, all the time. Some loans can be long-term payments with a fixed term, so you won't get rid of them too quickly. But avoid having too *many* loans, prioritize paying off short-term ones, and use sudden windfalls to reduce the longer ones.

And as far as possible, *please* don't take on new loans while you have existing ones running. If you bought a high-quality bedroom set on EMI, then you will not get poisoned eating off a cheap local-made dining table. You can replace it when the bedroom is paid off.

So, if you just took loan X to pay security deposit for your flat, then don't immediately take loan Y to buy a full furniture set. Better to keep X on short duration, focus on paying it off, and then taking Y, rather than having both running together for the next few years. It's always better to go for a *shorter* duration loan, as much as possible, as long as EMIs are manageable... and you can tell if they are, from budgeting.

For these type of 'normal' debts, the rate of interest is relatively lower - so it's possible to find other investment options, that give a better payout.

Then it makes more sense to put money into those investments, rather than blindly paying off every single loan first. You'll make (relatively) more than what you'll lose in interest payments, and sometimes you get really good opportunities that you shouldn't miss out on.

I'm not saying stop paying off the running loans; please keep that going. But you can also start making (some) investments in parallel, if you have the spare cash.

• • •

To Do

After credit cards, add up the other outflow - the loan repayments, any EMIs, buy-now-pay-later schemes, etc.

- List these down. Which bank, the total amount, the premium amount, due date of payment each month, interest, total amount remaining, time remaining. Penalties if any.
- Are any of them clearly more expensive than others? Can you close these earlier, especially if you can convert them into cheaper loans?
- When will each monthly payment end?
- When will you finally be totally free?

This will help bring some predictability into your cash flow - if you have visibility into how long a loan is for, you will have a better sense of when you can take on others in a planned way.

It also helps to understand if there are any available options for early payments, in case you want to repurpose some unexpected gains or bonus windfalls into those.

- Also, watch the total debt. If your EMIs are adding up to over 30% of your income, you're heading for, or are already in, a dangerous place.
- Avoid taking on any more debt or loans until this is reduced.

• • •

Tax Planning

The hardest thing in the world to understand is the income tax.

Albert Einstein

CHAPTER XXVIII

Pre–Tax Contributions: EPF and NPS

Some basics to remember for retirement savings.

Retirement saving is not sexy.

It's slow, gradual, over a very long time horizon. It usually happens in the background, with little interaction from you after the setup and minimal visibility. There are no fast moves, sudden jumps, overnight gains and dramatic falls. No drama, no excitement.

But there isn't *meant* to be.

These are part of the safe, secure, long-term, retirement backup plan. The primary plan is to make so much money with active investing, career growth, and smart decisions that you never need the backup plan, and *those* are the exciting things.

With excitement, comes risk.

Risk of *everything* going wrong, and the grand dream evaporating if circumstances went out of control - and nobody can predict or compensate for rare, but powerful, black-swan events that can happen without warning.

The purpose of a *backup* plan, however, is to get you out safe, and mostly unhurt, when catastrophe strikes - *not* to get you to your original, high-flying planned goal.

So, yes - these *won't* get you where you want, they may not even save you from inflation, but they *will* give you a **basic, fall-back position that you'll need for survival**, if everything falls apart.

Don't discout these, just because they're seen as *dadaji's* recommendation. They have a role; and it's always wise to understand whether that role has a place in your life's plan, before you discard it, or make any other major decisions.

And if you *do* see relevance, remember, these options require *literally* a lifetime commitment to deliver what they are supposed to. It's not something you can switch on and off at whim.

Luckily, they're not very demanding. Their purpose is to, reliably and safely, let you feed yourself, put a roof over your head, and have some basic lifestyle when your income stops, instead of having to resort to sitting on the local station steps, your trusty aluminum *katora* in hand.

Their job is to *grow slow*, but *stay safe*, free of market swings, companies going bust, geopolitics, regulations, and any other upheaval.

So, it's possible to have a 'start-and-forget; approach - switch it on, let it run, and forget about it apart from periodic checks.

The good news is, they don't take up much involvement, thought, effort, and even much money - but you do have to give them *time* to work.

So start early, leave it running, and you'll have either a safety net in place, if things go wrong, or a decent add-on if it all works out.

And yes, it comes *earlier* in the priority list - you have to be able to service this *before* more active investments.

• • •

EPF

EPF (*Employee Provident Fund*) is a single account, held with the government, where your employer has to contribute (pre-tax) an X amount, calculated against your salary, and your stated preferences. You do nothing except tell your HR how *much* you want to set.

This carries forward across employers, so when you change jobs, you have the option to either cash out (*taxes apply if cashed out before either 5 yrs in 1 place, or before retirement*), but take the better option, and carry it forward to your new employer.

It's got a fair interest rate as well, comparable to FDs.

EPF is mandatory, but you *can* choose to maximize or reduce contribution amount.

When you retire, leave the country permanently, be jobless for 2 months or more, or get disabled, you can opt to get it as a lump sum, or choose a part-withdrawal (*in some specific situations.*)

• • •

NPS

NPS (*National Pension Scheme*) is similar, with the primary differences being -

1. It's run by a pension fund manager, and the returns are market related, so they may vary. In a good economy, this means potentially better-than-FD returns. EPF returns are a fixed percentage.
2. It's more flexible, so you can choose to opt in or out, choose how much to contribute, and add top-ups if needed, or pause in dire situations.

3. When it matures (on retirement), you get a *part* of it as a lump sum, and the rest as an *annuity*, i.e. X payment paid out regularly each month for the rest of your life. This also ensures you don't blow the lot, the day you retire.

NPS is available for top-up post tax as well, completely optional, if you have some extra cash.

• • •

Another benefit - These two schemes are your chance to keep some of your hard-earned *kamai* out of the I-T department's greedy paws.

Whatever you earn, the government takes a cut as income tax, to build stuff you use, like roads, hospitals, schools, and a standing army. Whatever's left over, that's what you have with you to pay for your own *kharcha, and* invest for retirement.

But, if you do pre-tax NPS, that investment for retirement happens *before* the tax gets taken - so you're getting something extra, instead of paying it in taxes.

(*Why do these exist? If nobody saves for retirement, there will be millions of people sitting on train station steps with katoras in hand, making life difficult for themselves and everyone else - so the government wants you to save for retirement, and incentivizes you with these tax breaks.*)

Example - *Let's understand this better with 2 scenarios, pre and post tax.*

- *Scenario 1: Investing 10 after you get paid.*
  Salary 100. Income tax 25% = 25 taken. You get 75. Invest 10. Left: 65.
- *Scenario 2: Investing 10 before you get paid.*
  Salary 100. Invest 10. Left, 90. Income tax 25% = 22.5. You get 67.5. Left: 67.5

Now, if you're getting an extra 2.5 on every 100, while still keeping the same amount in investment, that adds up over time.

NPS usually caps out at 10% of salary, but it's still a decent amount, especially if the plan is to keep this *safe and unspendable until retirement.*

Remember, compounding?

The *longer* you do it, the *better* it works.

• • •

To Do

Find out -

- Does your salary have an NPS component?
- How much are you contributing to it?
- What's the max? Are you leaving anything behind by not maxing this out?
- What does that mean in tax savings? Do you have any room leftover in your tax saving components? (*see next chapter for details*)

Do you know, and have you recorded somewhere, your -

- PRAN ID
- EPF account
- UAN number

Are those accounts linked to your current mobile / email? (*Important, since these are create-and-forget, you may not have remembered to update a phone number or email if it changes.*)

- Can you access the account?
- Does it have the right nominee, address, etc?
- What's the return? Who's the fund manager?
- How many more years will you be working?
- In that time, how much will this NPS / EPF contribution add up to?
- If you withdraw it then, how much will you get? Is there any component you pay in tax?

What if you convert to an annuity?

- How will you get each month?
- Will that be enough, in the year 20__?

• • •

Recap

But before we get to tax saving, a recap of what we're doing, and where we've reached.

We've done all we could, around debt, critical payments, day-to-day life, and salary maximization.

Our *foundation's* sorted - now, we start building the superstructure, of *saving* and *investing*.

Remember the paycheck-to-paycheck cycle, inflation eating your future, compounding your savings at a high rate, to escape the trap?

Investing your savings gives you that high rate.

That's why we invest.

Depending *only* on a salary, with no savings... one day, you'll stop working - retired, fired, or injured - and there'll be nothing left to keep you alive. And likely, a mountain of debt as well.

Even if you *did* save, just savings alone is pointless - inflation grows, and the value of savings - and therefore, the sacrifices you made to get them - gets cut down to less and less.

By *investing*, you make the money you saved generate returns and grow itself.

This way, even if your wants increase, your savings still grow, even with the same income. The opposite - zero savings - means growing wants = growing debt, expensive and hard to escape.

With time, and enough saving + investing intelligently, they've grown to be more than your salary. **Financial Independence!**

• • •

CHAPTER XXIX

Tax Savers

Show of hands, **who likes giving away money?**

Every time you experience a power cut, a pothole, a long line, an official on lunch break, or a cop leaping out from behind a truck and fining you for helmetless biking - in fact, any form of government that infuriates you - you'll shake your fists at the sky and scream, *"Is this what I pay my taxes for?"*

I won't get into the debate of what you pay for, and what you get. But if you're particularly pissed off, you'll enjoy what comes next. We find out how *not* to pay taxes.

Ok... pay *less* taxes.

Relax, I'm not advocating grand tax evasion, black money, and double accounting. But I will help to legitimately avoid overpaying.

The tax structure and laws are a complex, convoluted system - and this means there can be a lot of confusion about how it works and what you pay. Let's get at least a basic awareness.

Remember, the government wants you to invest and save for various reasons, linked to their goals for betterment of society and country. So, they *incentivize* certain types of behavior. Retirement planning, women's empowerment, education, insurance, the environment.

These incentives come in the form of **tax savers** - i.e. if you save money linked to these goals, then you are rewarded by not having to pay as much taxes. These are tax exemptions, savers.

• • •

First option when you begin investing, look at the tax savers.

To put in ridiculously simple terms -

The government wants to do X, and spends money for it. It gets this money from taxes. When you also spend your money to achieve X, you're aligning your spending with the government. Now the government doesn't need to tax you to achieve X, because you did it already.

So, spending on X is exempted from being taxed, acting as an incentive for you.

What this means for you, is you telling your Finance - *"Bhai. I am putting X into all these tax exempt things. Please mark it in my salary, so the government doesn't cut tax on it"*. That's called an investment declaration, which you do once a year.

If you *don't* do this, your finance guys will naturally assume all your undeserved salary goes into a (taxable) flashy luxury lifestyle, full of wine, women, and song, and nothing contributed for the nation, and with a vengeance they'll accordingly cut the full tax.

You don't have to go overboard either; tax exemptions don't have to be a huge amount. There's specific *limits* on how much you can put into what kind of tax savers... and most of them you'd have already got, if you're taking insurance, paying certain loans, school fees, etc.

Tax exempt spends / investments are broken up into some **buckets**, (*the 80C, 80CC, 80D sections in your investment declaration and reflected in Form-16*) where you can **claim an exemption** upto a certain limit, each year.

- **80C & 80CCC**: PPF, EPF, school fees, life insurance, some pension funds, NSC, ELSS, home loan payments: up to 1.5 lakhs
- **80CCD**: NPS, up to 1.5 lakhs
- **80D**: Health insurance, up to Rs. 25,000
- And others, covering treatment of disabilities, education loans, first time home purchases, etc

If you're *already* doing these, just add up what you're paying in each section, and subtract it from the section limit. If there's a positive difference, then look for more investment options that offer this benefit.

If negative or zero, then buying another tax saver here will not save any more tax. Better to go for something else that can give better returns, or a saver in a different category.

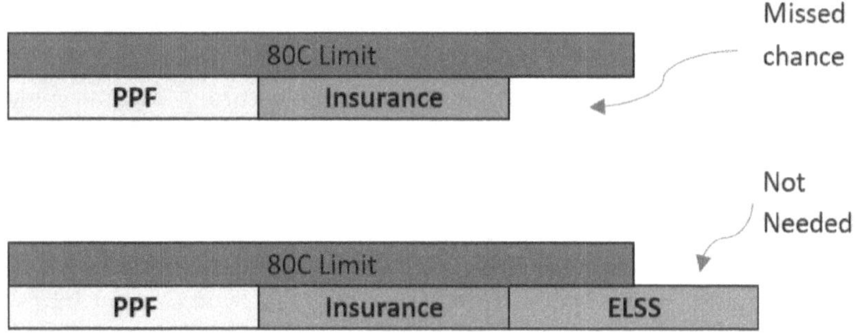

Are you optimizing your tax savers?

Example -

You're putting Rs. 50,000 in PPF, and Rs. 50,000 in Insurance. Total, Rs. 100,000.

80C has a limit of Rs. 1,50,000, so a full Rs. 50,000 is not being utilized. This will therefore be considered taxable income, and taxed. (Assuming a slab of 10%, Rs. 5,000 will be cut, leaving 40K to come to you... which you then invest).

Instead, use the opportunity to invest Rs. 50,000. Buy some ELSS, add some insurance, or increase PPF contributions.

If you do that, the full 1,50,000 is used in tax benefits, and you pay 5,000 less in taxes.

• • •

You have a *lot* of options to choose from, if you want to take the tax saving investments to their max limits - you could increase PPF / EPF / NPS contributions, buy ELSS mutual funds, participate in NSC schemes, put money in long-term FDs, increase life insurance, long term ULIPs, etc - see what aligns better with your goals and objectives, risk appetite, and personality. Some of them will apply to 80C, others to 80D, etc, and this will be explicitly mentioned - make sure you identify the right ones for each *category*.

Keeping an eye on the categories, also ensures you don't go overboard. Tax saving instruments like ELSS are usually good *because* you get that benefit of tax savings; Apart from that, they may not always be the *very* best investment option in the market. Once you hit each section limit, there's not much point in investing more, and other non-tax-savers may offer a better return.

Sorry - Car loans, personal loans, equity investments, and other similar investments, or any lifestyle expenses like groceries, travel, shopping, etc don't qualify as tax savers.

Tip: When you do go to buy these, try to time the payment to about 2-3 months before you have to give the *investment declaration* to your office (*usually in January.*) This way, all your receipts and proof of payment will have been received, and be ready when needed.

Another benefit of this timing is, it means you have to buy in the Aug-Oct period, usually a little bit after annual bonuses are given... giving you time to plan, and have ready cash.

You can still buy in the Jan-Mar period, but it's a hassle, scrambling for last-minute buys, declaring intended investments, then following up to furnish proofs.

• • •

To Do

- List out the tax saving components of your salary - 80C, 80D, etc
- List out the max limits of these as per your salary band.
- List out what are the current investments you are doing that are being claimed in each of these.
- Are there any *gaps*, i.e. room to add more?
- Are there any *overruns*, i.e. an investment made for tax savings that actually can't save any more tax? If yes, can you close this, and by when?
- When do you need to declare these to your organization?
- When do you receive proof for these? If you need to purchase more, when should you buy to ensure you get the details in time?

• • •

CHAPTER XXX

Should You Buy A House?

To be honest, I wasn't sure if I should include this. Home ownership is a huge decision, and probably one of the biggest purchases you'll ever make in your life.

This book's meant for people in the early stages of their career, 1-5 years ex.

Are you going to make a decision *that* big - as soon as you've just started working?

But I can't generalize. In some situations, buying your own house can be a logical decision; and I can't account for all of the unique circumstances around your earning level, local property prices, economic environment, future plans, estimated appreciation, and available financial support.

Some people have a lot on their plate already when they're starting out. Expensive cities where they work, high rent. A certain lifestyle. Planned and unplanned expenses. Dependents. Loans and repayments. Goals. Emergencies.

Others, don't.

Some people are simply *better placed* to buy a home early, compared to others.

The point is - I'm not saying *don't* buy; but think carefully.

Think about *why* you're buying, what you hope to get out of it, and what the impact on your life and savings is going to be.

· · ·

Most of all, think in terms of your *opportunity cost.*

If you *do* buy a house, especially early in life, you're committing a very large part of money to down payments, fees, and EMIs - money that could otherwise have been available for higher-risk, higher-return growth investing.

This higher-risk investing, don't forget, doesn't happen all by itself; it happens after you've taken care of your needs first. So if you have a lot of high-cost needs, you have less available to invest. Adding on a house EMI is a need. It reduces available investable money, perhaps to zero.

But, taking higher risks early is important too, because you have the *time* to make mistakes if you fail, and earn that much more if you succeed.

So maybe, consider adding on this particular need, only if you already have low needs. This still keeps a little bit available to invest.

If you have -

- *Family resources* available - a large sum for the down payment, a massive salary or income source, a sudden, big windfall gain, that solves the need to set aside savings or take loans for down payments and fees.
- *A place to stay* right now, that removes the need of rent payments, freeing them up for EMIs.
- *Familiarity with, and access to,* the location if in the same city, with local support and contacts helps avoid falling prey to scams or misinformation, leading to expensive delays or cancellations;
- If you have an expectation of building a long-term asset for the future, in a developing / growing city or town, where there will be a clearly understood, rational and reasonably likely possibility of significant appreciation...

If you have all this, *then* it can make sense.

But if you're buying it because your parents are pressuring you... or some friends are doing it... or you have a vague dream of a permanent beach vacation... or you watched too many realty-reality shows in exotic locales with exotic participants... *these are red flags.*

Going for a high-aspirational, high-cost home can become a *huge* weight to carry, and at the same time, it's *blocking other opportunities* to invest. All your money's going into the house EMIs. You'll never have the freedom to *experiment* with investing early in your career, or risk losing a job, because these large EMIs could drain your emergency fund very quickly. You'll always have to choose the safest possible option.

Even from an asset-appreciation perspective, property's not liquid. This means, if you need money quickly, you could be forced to sell *during a downturn...* and can lose a lot there. (*Plus, you can't sell 25% of a house, it's all or nothing.*)

On top of this, the whole headache of selling can take months... not exactly great for the nimbleness you need, in emergencies.

On the other hand, wait too long, and you'll miss opportunities - prices may rise, interest rates may go up, your life will change and other expenses will come in.

Most people will fall between these two extremes. You'll have to, dispassionately and unemotionally, evaluate where you are, and see what approach makes sense for you.

• • •

Basics to keep in mind -

- Don't look at a single project or builder, evaluate multiple options together.
- The banks can give max up to 80%-90% loans, but don't assume this means you have to pay only 10% down; the other charges of registration, stamp duty, interior build-out, new furniture, other miscellaneous can easily add up to equalling half or more of the original down payment.
- Max tenure for home loans offered is 20 years up till 60; so you can get this until age 40, then the available tenure starts going down (meaning EMIs will get higher, because you have to pay off in fewer years)
- Don't assume you can balance EMI with rental income, if you're renting it out; as a very basic thumb rule, EMI is 1% of total house cost. Rent will be much less than that, maybe just 20%-30% of EMI at best; during the periods between tenants, you'll still be paying those EMIs and maintenance, etc. And you still pay tax on rental income.
- If you are taking any advice, from anyone, make sure you know what their incentive is. A broker will be keeping his eye on the commission, so is more likely to push the builder who pays out more commissions. The salesperson will be focused on his month-end or year-end target, so will push to close quickly. You'll face a lot of pressure, given the size of the payout.
- A best friend might simply want you as a neighbor as well, and could tend to ignore your needs and push for their own building where you can can hang out together. Even family members may get overexcited (or jealous of some random cousin's purchase) and try to push the decision one way or another.

But in the end, it's going to be you who has to pay... and live with the consequences of the decision, so be sure you can filter out all this as much as possible.

It won't be easy, and it needs a high level of emotional maturity; be prepared for that.

And if it doesn't work out - budgets didn't fit, deals fell through, or the whole thing became too complicated - there'll be a period of *intense* disappointment.

That's *fine.*

Just don't let it put you off from trying again, next year. Better prepared. Ready.

• • •

CHAPTER XXXI

Recap: Your Personal Finance Journey Checklist

Let's see how we're progressing through the journey, shall we? How many more of the list have we been able to check off so far?

I have -

- Decided to take control of my personal finances
- Allocated a dedicated storage area for my documentation
- Understood the basic concepts of inflation, compounding, and risk
- Made a monthly budget, and follow it
- Familiarized myself with my salary structure and all benefits
- Purchased life insurance with payout of at least a year's earning
- Purchased personal health insurance with all critical riders
- Set up an emergency fund of at least 3 months' income
- Automated standard bill payments
- Cleared all my outstanding credit card and high-interest debts
- Reduced regular debts to under 30% of income
- Started contributing to a functional retirement account
- Utilized fully the tax saver components of my salary
- Deployed goal-based RDs
- Saved in at least one long-term FD
- Created a diversified mutual fund portfolio
- Invested in a diversified equity portfolio
- Explored 1-2 alternative investments
- Secured my digital footprint and credentials
- Started researching alternative income streams
- Planned the regular biannual physical checkup
- Vacationed at least once a year
- Reviewed each of the above in detail every 5 years.

Savings

The best time to start saving money, was yesterday. The second best time, is now.

Ancient Chinese Proverb

CHAPTER XXXII

Saving for the Short Term

I'll be honest. If you've got this far, boss, *hats off* to you.
After all this, you still have money left?! Brilliant.
So what you gonna do?

Now, you *could* spread it out on the bed and roll around on it, singing *paisa*-related songs. You could throw an epic party to end all parties, take a week's vacation, or buy every electronic gadget that you ever dreamed of owning as a child.

Sure, *do* that. But don't do it with *all* the cash.

Take *some* - as much as you like - and set up a monthly RD, set to convert into FD on maturity. This should be your *default* setting. If you think of something better to do, anytime, break the FD. But keep the RD going, because that brings in the *discipline* of doing a mandatory save each month.

Yes, an FD is as old-school as it gets. It's slow, boring, very fuddy-duddy, and once you adjust for inflation and taxes, just about keeping your head above water. We're not growing our money yet - don't worry, we'll come to that too - it's about *protecting* what you've saved, and building habits.

Doing an FD is like a Level Zero of saving, where the point is not to save an X amount, but -

1. To build the habit of saving;
2. To save in a way that's regular, and sustainable;
3. To safeguard your leftover cash in a place that's not easily spendable;
4. To build an amount that is reasonably significant.

How much, you ask? What if there is something that comes up, and I can't keep paying that RD amount each month?

Don't worry, that won't happen.

You know why? Because you have your budget already set.

You already know (roughly) what you need to pay in expenses, you already know you have an emergency reserve. Everything left over after that, it's either blow-up money, or save-for-future money.

If you ever start running short of save-for-future money, you can cut back the blow-up money (*which should always be optional and non-recurring.*)

• • •

Once you get into the habit of doing this, and can maintain it, Then we can move to Level One.

The Goal-Based RD.

This approach is a useful system of short-term savings, used for paying *big* payments (like annual insurance premims, or other annual investments.) These payments are major, non-monthly, and can't easily be absorbed into the monthly salary. When they hit, you're left scrambling to somehow scrape enough funds together to make that payment.

But you have an advantage - you know exactly *when* they need to be paid, and *how much.*

Here's how you tackle them.

Start setting up RDs that mature at the time that the payment is due. This effectively converts that big annual payment into a small regular monthly one, lets you adjust in a smaller amount in the monthly budget, and gives an ok interest payout.

Example -

Say, you have to pay Rs. 1,00,000 in some fees in Apr.

It's now Aug. You have 8 months left.

Start an RD of Rs. 100,000 / 8 = Rs. 12,500 for 8 months, right now. You will get your Rs. 1L exactly on time, when you need it.

Then, once it's paid, immediately create a new RD of Rs. 1,00,000 / 12 = Rs. 8,333 (for 12 months), starting that Apr. This'll give you the same amount next year.

Repeat the process, for each identified major payment.

If the fees increase, you only have to come up with the difference amount at the time (or use the interest), and set your next RD amount to factor in the increased fees.

Important - remember to *restart the RD*, every time it finishes. It'll be hard the first time, because you have to have enough money to pay the first fee, plus set up the RD for the next time. The timings can be complicated, and you'll be struggling with excel sheets, calendars, and calculations.

But once you have it up and running, it will run like *clockwork.*

You'll be *amazed* at how much peace of mind this brings. No more sacrificing a weekend trip or fancy celebration, or desperately waiting for some uncertain bonus amount or tax refund to come, just so you can pay X.

Don't do it all together. Start with the biggest payments, then gradually set it for smaller ones, as many as you're comfortable with. If your bank lets you nickname RDs, great, otherwise keep a list of which RD # is for what payment. This is important, because you don't want to accidentally mix up payments, spend the difference, then fall short.

It also adds a safety margin, in case of emergencies. If there's ever a time you need a lot of money, immediately, you always have the option of delaying starting the renewed RD for a 2-3 month period, then restarting with a slightly higher amount to cover the difference. You'll have enough of a run-up before your due date, to be able to compensate.

Remember, we *haven't* yet got into long-term saving for the future. We're on the last part of making sure our current expenses - especially the non-monthly, often-overlooked ones - can be anticipated, and met. These are big, irregular, and hard to handle if you haven't prepared.

What many people do, is link it to windfalls - *get a bonus, buy a policy* - but that takes all the joy out of achieving and enjoying that bonus, and it's risky - one year your bonus is delayed or missed, you're *screwed*.

• • •

To Do

Phase One - the test: can you save regularly?

- Look up your budget tracker sheet (after you've been following it for a few months) and check how much, on average, is left over each month.
- Set up a short-term RD of that amount, or slightly less. This is a proof-of-concept - you're doing this to first establish if you'll be able to do this sustainably or not. You don't want to be breaking RDs and screwing up the whole planning in future, if you start falling short, or finding there are emergencies or situations you didn't factor in.
- When the RD matures, keep a little to treat yourself for a job well done, and put the rest into a long-term FD. Then forget about it.

Phase Two - the setup: can you service annual payments?

- Make a list of all the large annual payments, with amount and date
- How many months away from today are they? Mark all that are at least 6.
- For each, divide the amount by the number of months remaining
- List these down in a table, with rows for items, and columns for key details and months, with the RD amount of each item per month.
- Add the total per column. Is this amount available as surplus each month after regular expenses? (*Relax, it usually won't be. That's why you need to selectively pick the critical ones first.*)

Once you've picked out the critical ones, set up those RDs.

Phase Three - the ongoing annual process

- Every time an RD matures, pay the due amount
- *Immediately* create a new RD of the required amount next year / 12. This will be lower, allowing you to expand the process to other big payments.

• • •

CHAPTER XXXIII

Dream Goals

This same logic also applies for major 'dream' goals - a big purchase, a down payment, a holiday, some major known event - if you know *when* it is needed, and *how much* you need, setting up an RD in advance lets you meet that day with a ready pile of cash.

Isn't that better than having to fork out a chunk of your savings, or breaking long-term FDs?

Even worse - without this ready amount, you'll end up being forced to take on loan EMIs, and pay more in fees and interest. (*This typically happens with flight tickets and white-good purchases, because the easy-financing guy sits right in the shop, ready to loan you whatever you want for that impulse buy, or the airline's website has EMI options tied to most bank cards.*) These are RDs in reverse - instead of earning interest, you pay fees, and instead of saving in advance, you pay more later.

That also adds the unpleasantness of paying for something after it's all over, spoiling both the experience, and the memory, with repayment-stress misery.

Don't forget - in planned RDs, you are earning interest, not paying it like in loans!

Warning - don't attempt this with equities or mutual funds. They may earn higher interest & returns, but they're market-linked, so their value will fluctuate; and you don't want to hit the payment day when the market is down, and be forced to sell at a loss (*the payment amount and date is fixed, and won't wait for the market to recover even - if you're sure it will*).

What you need is something stable, reliable, low-risk, and predictable - hence RDs.

Reiterating -

This same logic also applies for major 'dream' goals - a big purchase, a down payment, a holiday, some major known event - if you know when it is, and how much you need, setting up an RD in advance lets you meet that day with a ready pile of cash.

Isn't that better than having to fork out a chunk of your savings, or breaking long-term FDs?

Even worse - without this ready amount, you'll end up being forced to take on loan EMIs, and pay more in fees and interest. (I've seen this happen most often with flight tickets and white-good purchases, because the easy-financing guy sits right in the shop, ready to loan you whatever you want for that impulse buy, or the airline's website has EMI options tied to most bank cards.) These are RDs in reverse - instead of earning interest, you pay fees, and instead of saving in advance, you pay more later.

That also adds the unpleasantness of paying for something after it's all over, spoiling both the experience, and the memory, with repayment-stress misery.

Don't forget - in planned RDs, you are *earning* interest, not paying it like in loans!

Warning -*don't* attempt this with equities or mutual funds. They may earn higher interest & returns, but they're market-linked, so their value will fluctuate; and you don't want to hit the payment day when the market is down, and be forced to sell at a loss (the payment amount and date is fixed, and won't wait for the market to recover even - if you're sure it will).

What you need is something stable, reliable, low-risk, and predictable, hence RDs.

• • •

Goal-based RDs are *not* meant to grow your savings.

They're meant to *regularize* and *safeguard* your spare cash, so you can meet large, recurring, annual (or longer) payments, without paying extra in interest, fees, and charges. They're a way to control and reduce cost, not increase return.

I'm deliberately saying annual or longer planned, because this approach won't work for -

1. Sudden unexpected expenses - that's what the emergency fund is for.
2. Planned expenses very far (5+ years) in the future - an RD approach works, but with a longer run-up time, you can consider higher-risk, higher return options, since you'll have time to take profits at the right time beforehand.

If you're meeting monthly expenses, have insurance and an emergency fund, then goal-based RDs are only a way to meet planned annual expenses.

We haven't come to grow-your-money investments yet.

The only thing you'll need to wrap your head around, is this.

This approach requires preplanning, attention to detail, and patience.

It's not an impulse buy; you'll need to have thought of what you're going to spend on, and how much, well enough in advance that you can set up saving for it. Anticipate future festival discounts as well as reasonable price increases.

This doesn't mean you lock in the choice of specific purchase. If you know you want to take a big holiday with the gang next year, you don't have to choose the flights and set the itinerary today. You just have to fix a date (*when* you'll need the money) and set the budget (*how much* money you'll need).

Then you put the process in place, let the savings accumulate, and do your selection, bookings, and tickets purchase when the time comes. Same for the next flagship iPhone, Tods bag, or car down payment.

Another benefit - this also frees you from the temptation of succumbing to urgent marketing 'offers', scam artists, and hasty decisions. You know what you want, and when, and have a budget and plan in place. You can wait for it.

If you don't know what, when, and for how much, then you're tempted to buy anything, anytime, for any amount.

• • •

CHAPTER XXXIV

Bonuses and Windfalls

We've mentioned bonuses before. This could be a sales incentive, a target achieved, merger payout, some company-milestone generosity, Diwali or Christmas bonus.

You could win a lottery, receive an inheritance, sell a property (or a car, or art), or cash out your eSOPs. You could have got a lot of cash gifts on your 21st birthday, engagement, or wedding.

What do you do with it?

Listen. I'll *irritate* you now, by taking the exact *opposite* stance to everything I've said so far.

Don't save carefully, and put this all into FDs and stuff.

Spend.

Why?

You've been working hard, cutting costs, saving cash, taking control of your life.

You *deserve* a little reward.

The point of all the planning and budgeting, is to free these sudden gains from being used in regular, life-as-usual stuff.

Dong the pre-planning also keeps you free from the trap of waiting for a bonus to pay off something - because you should *never plan to spend money, that you haven't yet got.*

There the danger comes, when you end up committing money that never showed up, leaving you well and truly *fucked.*

Don't blow *all* of it together, though - put just a little aside for later, and treat yourself with the rest.

There's another reason I'm saying this, though, because I'm fairly confident - once you've gone through the process of sorting out your basics, planned for the future, and have decent financial habits in place - you, yourself, won't be *able* to blow up the bonus on some random crap.

Sure, buy that 50-inch tv, the PS5, the KTM. Take the Vietnam holiday. After a point, you'll find that your own new-found sense of discipline will be holding you back, stopping you from going on a mad spending spree. In the past, you would've burned through everything in a matter of days. No more.

Hey, look at that - in spite of everything, you've become *responsible!*
I'm sorry I did that to you.

Don't forget - these kind of sudden windfall gains *aren't tax-free* - unless it's a bonus that your company has already cut the income tax on - so don't get caught with your pants down during tax filing, and be forced to scramble and get that 30% for taxes... if you've already spent the entire bonus. Any windfall's true value should be counted post-tax. Calculate and lock away that tax component first.

Later on, I'll talk about SWPs. If you have a sudden unexpected amount of cash and no specific plan to invest it, consider an SWP to spread it out.

$$\bullet \ \bullet \ \bullet$$

Investing

Don't work for money. Make it work for you.

Robert Kiyosaki

CHAPTER XXXV

Stable, Long-Term Investing

We've set our basic money habits in order, and controlled our cash flow. Critical needs are met; emergencies are planned for; big payments are in control; and we've maximized what we could be making.

Everything so far, has been *basic hygiene. This* is where it begins to get *interesting.*

What we have now, is the cash left over for investing.

Why do we invest?

It all comes back to the first thing we started with. *Inflation.*

A few generations ago, you started out modestly, worked hard, spent a little, and saved dutifully. You were rewarded with a comfortable, relaxed life, peace of mind, and time to spend with family and hobbies, ending into a simple, easy, low-stress retirement.

This was possible, not just because you had few choices and little societal pressure, (though it helped!) but *because the cost of living did not change* much, year to year. It's why stability worked, and why those stable government jobs were prized.

Today, the same approach is a *recipe for disaster.* As India started getting more connected with the global economy, more liberalized, and the economy started growing faster, inflation started rising as well.

Costs have now grown *much* higher, and today, there are far greater opportunities to spend... so money is flowing out of your hands like never before.

But not spending (and simply saving) is dangerous as well - because rapidly-rising inflation is eating those savings.

Even if you spend nothing, you still end up with nothing... and without even new experiences and possessions along the way.

You need to find a way to keep *ahead* of inflation, and your bank's 3.5% savings account interest simply isn't going to cut it. Even your 7% FD and PPF will *just* about keep pace.

To get out of this running-in-place trap, you'll need to find ways to get ahead of that inflation rate.

By the way, do you even know what the real inflation rate is?

If not, google it now. Easy enough to find. Lots of learned economist types, finance ministers, and experts with projections will present it.

• • •

Unfortunately, those are not always reliable.

Think of what you spend on basics, and how that has changed over the last year or two. Fuel, groceries. Eating out. A beer. Your kids' fees. What the maid is asking for per month.

It doesn't seem to match, does it?

In your gut, you know that things are getting costlier, faster than you can manage.

If you can find an old grocery receipt, repeat the order from the same place. *That's* the real inflation figure, because it's the one that hits you specifically, according to your actual spending habits.

Ask your grandfather how he ran a household of dependent parents, children, and random siblings/cousins on a monthly salary of Rs. 800.

Think of your situation today. Your current salary, and how much it's been increasing year-on-year.

Think of how this will project forward a couple of years, decades.

Think, if this meets the rising costs.

Then get scared. *Very* scared.

The truth is, your salary will *not* keep pace. Inflation is relentless, and persistent, now. Even if you do absolutely nothing (lifestyle-wise) beyond what you do today, you might barely get away with it - but as you grow, you'll be adding on more expenses.

Living is geometric growth, but Life... is *exponential.*

It *will* get away from you, if you let it.

• • •

You invest so you change your situation from Fig 1 to Fig 2 below. Staying dependent on a slowly-growing, incremental salary will not let you keep pace with life's sudden movements - not just inflation, but larger blocks of expenses that get added as life changes.

Life gets away from you if you let it

Anticipating these, and building in similar exponential jumps, coupled with a steady investing strategy to outpace inflation, is the only way to ensure you don't fall behind.

Remember, on top of all this - one day, your *income* will stop, too. If you're lucky, not for a long time, but stop, it will - and you need to be ready when it does.

So, we need to find ways to make your savings grow, the same exponential way.

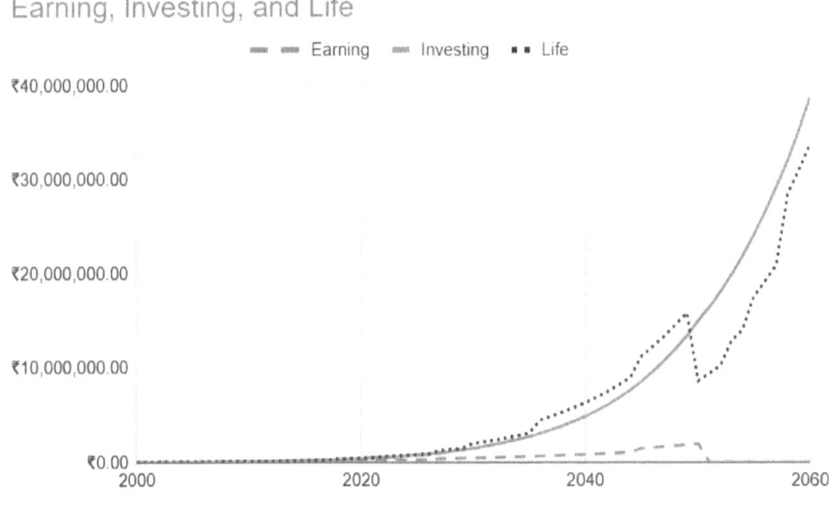

Investing vs Life Expenses vs Earnings

This chart above is a thought experiment.

The (dashed) **Earning** line is your *salary*, growing at a steady small % year on year. (*I've considered this as separate from investing - i.e. this is the regular money-come-in, money-go-out process.*)

The (dotted) **Life** line is *expenses life hits you with.* Those rise faster, and in jumps - further education, marriage, kids, house, kids schools, kids higher education, your own health, parents' health... not only does stuff get more expensive, but new, big, *heavy* stuff gets added. If you tried to match Earnings to Life, you'll run out money very fast.

That sudden drop two-thirds of the way, around 2050? That's when you retire, earnings go to zero... and hopefully, a good part of your expenses as well. You can now move to a cheaper location, have your own place so no rent, stop the commute, your kids are now self-sufficient, etc. You're still going to have expenses, sure - food, general living, medical expenses, but they should be less than before.

But they'll still rise.

But the (solid) **Investing** line, that's the one that's got to stay on the up and up, because this is the money that's going to *keep* working for you, even when you stop earning - and if you started right, and stuck with it, it's got the potential to become this self-powering engine, that grows and builds itself. That's the *only* one that can keep pace with rising costs, and beat the.

And building that rising line, *that* is the objective of investing.

● ● ●

The last thing before we jump off, remember **Diversification**.

Diversification is **risk management**.

Everything fails, sooner or later. Every plan, every strategy, every road taken or not taken, will run into something unexpected it cannot handle, and collapse.

This will also be true of your financial plans, and the things you do to earn, save, and grow your money. Some are safer than others, but *nothing is 100%.*

Diversification is a way to make sure that you have 10 things going on, where only 1, or max 2, can fail at a time. You'll have to have 8 more to keep you going.

Diversify the plans, the instruments, the areas you invest in. Do different things, use different products, and distribute them out. If there are options within them, spread that out as well.

Some won't work out, and that's fine.

Some will.

It's *uncomfortable*. It's not a simple, set-once-and-forget approach. It requires you to stay on top of your investing, track what's working, what new products have hit the market, what new ways of investing are now available. You'll need to do this constantly, always learning, always experimenting. It will need a *lot* of effort.

But the alternative? It's the gamble-everything approach. You *could* get *very* lucky, sure.

But the outcome, if you get *unlucky*?

The End. Lights out. Pack up.

How many times in the course of an entire lifetime are you going to keep getting lucky?

• • •

To Do

- Create an excel.
- Put the *salary* you have today, and project it over the next 40 years (or as long as you intend to keep working) with a standard X% growth year-on-year. Feel free to add some jumps - promotions, job changes.
- Put the *expenses* you have today, and project them using inflation in the same way. Add in the expected life events - partner, kids, home, sickness. Be realistic. Remember to keep going for a longer time, unless you plan to die the day you retire.
- Put the *savings* you are able to set aside today, and project it forwards- this time using a decent average rate of return. Add the occasional boost along the way - a bonus reinvested, etc.
- *Plot* each one on a time-vs-amount graph.

You'll get a set of lines that look like the chart described.

Do you see how, once income stops, expenses very rapidly catch up and exceed savings? When those lines cross, you'd better have grateful children to support your ass, otherwise you're out on the footpath at that point.

But do you also see, how even a relatively small amount of saved money invested carefully, can continue to grow and deliver returns outpacing the salary itself, and keep going forever?

What's the amount and % return you found, that can do this?

The same calculation will be there in the worksheet, but don't cheat - try and find this yourself first. Discovery is always retained more viscerally than any explanation, however good.

• • •

CHAPTER XXXVI

Mutual Funds

Let's start with the basics.

MFs are like *outsourcing your equity investing.* Say, you want to invest, but have no idea what stocks to pick, when to buy/sell, what to drop or pick up, and what to hold onto.

All you have, is a rough idea in your head that you'll invest, maybe a preference for some sector or strategy... but nothing more.

In that case, MFs are an ideal starting point.

So, what's a mutual fund?

Basically a way to buy a group of stocks, according to some categorization. There can be MFs for -

- only blue-chip companies (*good largecaps*);
- focusing on *smaller, faster-growing* companies (*midcaps and smallcaps*);
- following and replicating *top companies* overall or a sector (*index funds*);
- focusing on *non-Indian* companies, like in US or China, or global (*offshore*);
- stocks of companies according to specific *themes*, like IT, BFSI, Infra, etc (*thematic*);
- a mix of *different* sizes, (*flexi-cap or multi-cap*);
- funds that buy *debt* instruments, instead of stocks, where the goal is to keep money *safe,* rather than aggressively grow;
- and there can even be, Russian-doll-style, funds that consist of other funds. (*FoF*)

So which ones are right for us?

Before we can answer that, we need a little bit more knowledge.

• • •

How do they work?

A MF company decides on an idea (like one of the above), and hires a smart, focused, and financially savvy *fund manager* to run the fund. This guy will come with training, experience, education, and he will spend *every waking moment* thinking how he can deliver good returns from the fund.

He'll do his research and choose what to buy or sell, and when; how much risk to take, and how to hedge and safeguard bets, day in and day out... all so *you* don't need to.

All *you'll* need to do, by buying units of this fund, is give him some of your money to use in this task. Many other folks will give as well, so this guy now has a giant sack of money to use... for buying up what he feels are the best stocks in that theme (this giant sack money and equities is called the *AUM, i.e. Assets Under Management*).

Then, as the fund manager works his magic, identifying and picking good companies that appreciate in value, the total value of the stocks held in the fund overall goes up, which means *the value of the individual units of the fund, also goes up.* When you decide to cash out, you sell your units, and get back whatever was the value of those units at the time of selling.

You want more units? You give him more money.

A good fund manager will make smarter decisions, pick better stocks with better timing, and make the overall fund value increase more. Bad ones will not, the fund will grow poorly.

For this service, the company running the fund charges you a small percentage.

Almost everyone looks only at which MFs have done well in the past (i.e. given best returns) while choosing, but this *isn't* a guarantee.

Instead, look at other things that indicate good health in a fund.

- The size (AUM) which will tell how big it is (indicating how stable) and how liquid (meaning how easy to buy/sell);
- Benchmark comparison, i.e. is it doing better or worse than the market, or industry average;
- Expense ratio, and entry / exit loads, i.e. how much fees it charges;
- Who is the fund manager (expertise, experience, tenure);
- Diversification (i.e. is it investing broadly across different sectors, companies, and classes, or overly dependent on a few);
- and 3rd-party ratings, like Morningstar.

While this may sound complicated, making it a quick **checklist** can help make decisions and comparisons faster, and the overall decision more reliable.

One important fact - while you *can* buy MFs as a one-off purchase, MFs are typically taken as an **SIP** (a *Systematic Investment Plan*) for at least a year, and can go on indefinitely. Ideally, a 3-5 year tenure is good to start with - it'll give you flexibility, and not lock you into a bad decision.

Be aware of the risks.

MFs are a bundle of *stocks*. Stocks go up and down with the market, as economic conditions change. The skill of a fund manager lies in being able to drop the stocks that fall, and buy the stocks that rise. But if the market *overall* goes down - during recessions, wars, natural disasters - where *every* stock is losing value, then *no* fund manager in the world can make money magically appear.

In this scenario, the value of the units of the fund you own will also go down, possibly wiping out all your profits, and maybe even giving you back less than what you put in.

There are *no guaranteed returns* or safety, like in FDs - if you chose a bad fund manager, or the economy tanked, you can lose even the initial amount you invested.

On the other hand, if things are going ok, you can expect a (much) better return than the safer, guaranteed ones like FDs.

• • •

Allocating your investments in Mutual Funds

At first, go for a **standard index fund**, like a Nifty50 or Sensex tracking fund. This will be stable, relatively safer, and as long as the economy is doing well, this should stay at pace, or better. As you add others, make sure this is still the largest component of the total. Keep checking this, and periodically increase it, or add new ones in the same category, if you find better options.

While starting out, gradually adjust the mix of *which* funds you're buying, and *how much* you're investing by some broad goals. The stages below are not a recommendation, but an illustration, of how to think about structuring your MF portfolio. Start small, and readjust as you feel more comfortable with the regular investments and are in control of the process.

- **Stage 1:** 100% largecap index
- **Stage 2:** At least 50% largecap index, 30 midcap, 20 smallcap.
- **Stage 3:** At least 40% largecap index, 20 midcap, 20 smallcap, 10 thematic, 10 others

Once you've got your feet wet and familiarized yourself with the processes, with a basic index fund, start exploring other categories. Add some **midcaps** and (a little) **smallcaps**, for higher risk, higher returns. In a good growing economy, these can go up a lot, but also fall quite a bit if the market does badly.

Next, add **thematic** funds, if you want to bet on what sectors are going to do well. It's a chance to ride on a specific sector (like IT, Pharma, Infra, etc) doing better than the average, but you *will* need to research on *why* that is, what's the expected timeline, etc.

Over time, *experiment*. Diversify further, consider offshore funds that give a chance to invest in non-Indian stocks - think about what economies and sectors are likely to be doing well, and take this chance to be a part of that. But remember this is riskier, because you're not familiar with the environment and the ground reality.

The thing to keep in mind - have a mental picture of what the mix should be like, and don't go overboard chasing every new offering or product that comes out. The blue-chip largecap component of your portfolio exists to bring stability and protect from sharp downturns; don't forget to keep this growing in parallel, as your overall investments increase.

Some MFs also offer *tax saving benefits*, like ELSS funds; there are also ULIPs, which give insurance + investment options. Each has advantages and disadvantages; MFs are cheaper and offer better returns because 100% is invested, whereas ULIPs put a portion towards insurance, but give more flexibility in the investment strategy. ULIPs also tend to have more fees and charges, but the returns may be more tax-free than a maturing ELSS. There will be a lot of variations; please research thoroughly.

These options should be considered only if there's a specific opportunity to *reduce tax* by investing in ELSS or ULIP, or if you feel you're *short on insurance,* and want to top up. Otherwise, try to keep the different instruments separate according to purpose. If you want insurance, buy insurance, and if you want to invest, then invest. Trying to do both, will get you neither.

• • •

How-to:
To begin with MFs,

1. Open a **demat account** in any investing firm with the standard KYC process
2. Set up an **ECS mandate** authorizing withdrawals from your bank
3. **Research & identify** which MFs you want to invest in, and
4. **Schedule** and set up an SIP.

This'll automatically deduct the SIP amount from your account on the set date (*pick something early in the month so the cash hasn't been spent, but not too early in case salary is delayed or there's a bank holiday / weekend on the 1ˢᵗ*).

• • •

The key advantage MFs offer, is a **fill-it, shut-it, forget-it approach.**

Pick a decent set of funds, start your SIPs, then sit back and relax. You *don't* need to obsessively follow them, you don't need to make daily evaluations and decisions like a day-trader, and you don't need to learn an entirely new, complex skillset like equity picking.

You've outsourced all that to your fund manager.

MFs do their best when they're allowed to run a while, so the only thing you'll need to have, is *patience.* An annual evaluation should be good enough to figure out if you picked a good fund, and take a call whether to stay invested or pull out (*and think long and hard before pulling out - is the fund doing badly, or the economy?*) Pulling out too early hurts the long-term averaging benefit a regular SIP offers; don't take that decision too fast.

This slow, systematic approach also protects you from the worst mistakes of investing - making rash, emotional decisions in panic, based on half-assed knowledge and misleading information.

• • •

To Do

- Research up on what platforms are good for MFs. Look for ease of use, fees, safety, stability. Avoid spreading across multiple platforms without a clear reason - makes it hard to track.

  - Open a demat account, link your bank.
  - Setup an ECS mandate to enable SIPs.
  - Set a target amount that can be invested each month.

- Plan a **time goal** - minimum one year, but ideally, between three to five years at least. Record that date.
- Research and set a realistic goal for expected gains. It needs to be **better than your FDs.** Record that as well. This'll help you understand if you're getting to your goals.
- Over time, spread the investment amount into some broad categories by adding more funds. If you're starting out, **stick to the largecap index funds.**
- **Research** at least 3 - 5 best mutual funds in each category you want to invest in. Do *not* go for just the best past performance; look at ratings, size of the AUM, fees, popularity (meaning future liquidity), minimum SIP amount, and likelihood of long-term stability.
- Basis this, pick one in each of the categories you selected and set up the SIPs.
- Each year, evaluate if any SIPs need to be stopped, and learn about how long-term cycles, economy and geopolitical influence affect market performance.
- Whenever you have to add new investments, ensure the overall diversification is maintained. As with any investment, the majority should be a 'safer' category and the higher-risk, a lower split.

• • •

CHAPTER XXXVII

Intermission 4

Saumya walked grimly into office, already (it was just 9:30) feeling itchy and grimy. She'd been on the road - and train, and share cab - since early morning, her commute periodically punctuated by her boss's never-fail Whatsapps - what happened with X? Did you send Y? Have you heard back from Z? You know this is critical! - that had begun firing off almost as soon as she was awake.

The Old Man was hyperactive, bored, living in constant fomo, completely incompetent, and long past the age at which he should have retired, or preferably, died. With nothing better to do, this insecurity would manifest in constant messaging, meetings, gossip, and regular post-work 'socializing' that would turn into GoT-level political minefields for everyone present.

Leaving her Baba-Azam-era laptop to squeak & whirr in its 5-minute bootup, she headed to the pantry. Neha and Bharti - the only two somewhat sane colleagues, and therefore, her best friends in office - looked up from the coffee machine.

"OMG, what's that face?"

"Arre, can't you guess. Babaji started, already?"

She sighed, nodded, grabbing a cup. "I'm so fed up with this place. I don't want to deal with this shit anymore."

"So when are you moving?"

"Are you even looking?"

She was looking - had been looking, in fact, for a few months. Linkedin, consultants, contacts, anything she could try. Somehow nothing was working - either she was too senior in a too-niche role, or in the wrong industry for the time, or her CV was missing whatever unknown keywords were the current flavor of the season - she had no idea why she was drawing a blank, everywhere.

"Ya, I will. Soon. I hope."

"Just quit, babe. Take a break, do that Vipassana silence thing you want, then get back and look properly."

And that thought was so nice, so viscerally tempting, she lost herself in the daydream for a minute.

Ding!

Reality crashed down, with a payment-due sms.

"*No re. I can't - my idiot husband is still chilling at home, and one of us has to pay bills, no? Where I can just quit, like that?*"

"*Oh, how's his investing thing going? Must be nice, no - no boss, no office, just sit at home and do trading fulltime? I wish I could do that...*"

"*It's ok... not great, but chal raha hai.*"

And that was a lie. It wasn't doing great. It wasn't even doing break-even average. Abhishek had been 'playing the market' for a couple of months now, living off a continuous stream of Youtube, Telegram and his MBA buddies' Whatsapp groups.

He had - at first - made a decent, not more-than-salary level, but an okay amount of profit. That had somehow led to his getting into a fight with his manager, walking out in a huff, and declaring he was launching into a full-time day-trading career.

"*After all,*" *he'd confidently announced, ignoring her aghast looks,* "*If I can make that much part-time, then I'll bloody clean up if I do this dedicated, right?*"

He hadn't cleaned up. At first he'd first lost a little... then some more. That triggered a panic, and he'd tried to recover with increasingly riskier, leveraged plays - and within one bad week, got wiped out, burning through his entire full & final settlement. He'd been on the verge of cashing out his EPF to keep going, before she'd stopped him by threatening to walk out of the marriage, or break his head, or both.

Now he sat sulking at home, alternating between wildly improbable business ideas, or grumpy, ill-tempered freelancing projects, refusing to talk about anything career-linked. She hoped he'd settle down soon... and get a damn job.

But until then, she would have to postpone the car, cut back all shopping, keep her head down, and carry on. No hope in hell of quitting now... not at least until something much better came along.

The phone rang.

Her stomach clenched.

"*Are you not reading my messages?*"

"*Good morning, sir. I'm here, I was-*"

"*Haan, haan, good morning, now stop yakking in the canteen and come fast, we are about to start the morning catchup. Why you're so late? You have your updates ready? No, you listen. Do I have to remind how very important this meeting is - Amitji and Gulabji are personally watching the project and have to be in the loop. About everything, you understand? Come fast.*"

"*2 minutes, sir.*"

Saumya took a deep breath, burnt her tongue on the coffee, settled her face into blank neutrality and walked to the conference room.

Just one more day, like every other.

Until something better came along...

CHAPTER XXXVIII

Stocks

This is one you'll be pretty familiar with, thanks to all the movies, shows, stories, memes, myths and legends bouncing around pop culture the last ten years. Equities - or shares, stocks - have gained a popularity - and notoriety - very different from most financial or investment instruments.

Stocks, or **Equities**, are where you buy shares of a public, listed company. The price of shares goes up or down, depending on how well the company is doing (or believed to be doing, now or later).

You buy it when it's low, you sell it when it's high.

You don't buy it if it's going to fall, or sell it if it's going to rise.

Thus, profit.

'But, but,' you say, *'How will I know when it's going higher or lower? I can't see the future!'* That's right... but neither can anybody *else*. Not Warren Buffet, not Ray Dalio, not Rakesh Jhunjhunwala, not any influencer-finfluencer, Telegram group, financial publication, or website.

(*The senior management of the company in question probably can, but they get very heavily fined / go to jail if they buy or sell basis that awareness - that's insider trading.*)

So how do these stock gurus - and you - decide *what* and *when* to buy or sell?

Unfortunately, that answer is boring, difficult... and not the one you're looking for.

They decide with a *lot* of research, studying, thinking, hard work... and a 1% intuition, that only comes with *years* of experience.

And even then, they're often wrong.

The line between success and failure lies in being wrong *just a little less*, than everyone else.

When a company goes public, they make shares available to the retail investor (i.e. you) via the stock market. Buying a share(s) gives the investor a part-ownership of the company, and the company gets a bunch of cash to use in growing their business.

If the company does well, the shares become more valuable, increasing in price. Having shares makes you a part-owner, so you get a share of profits as dividends, or choose to sell your part-ownership to someone else who believes it'll go even higher.

The goal - mostly - is to pick the companies that are likely to do well, buy their shares early while they're cheap, then sell them later when they increase in price (appreciate). That's it. *Easy.*

And to achieve this, there are a host of different strategies deployed.

• • •

Basics of investing strategy

No.

Go and buy a book or ten, do a course.

I'm *not* going to be telling you here about investing strategy and stock picking.

It's too complex a topic, too large, diverse, and technical to include right now.

But - I can talk about a general approach.

And I'm afraid my approach is a slow, steady, careful, and extremely boring approach, where there won't be any overnight success, massive lottery-win gains, or thrilling, nail-biting tension. What there *will* be... will be long, boring, repetitive work, lots of numbers and excel sheets, research, and reading.

Sorry.

Learning to invest will involve a couple of core understandings - some focused and technical, some general-awareness related, and even a sense of your own personality and goals.

It'll involve learning to read a company's financial data, balance sheet, annual report, past performance, financial concepts, understanding their debt, revenue, costs and profits, identifying trends, correlating economic, regulatory, sociopolitical and geopolitcal factors, figuring out key performance indicators and their implications, the company's business model, competition, how it fits in the market, and just for some extra fun, impact of the weather, climate change, rumours, and mass hysteria.

You should know how and why all this fits together, before you start.

Until then - well, you can still start, but the quality of your decision will be based 90% on guesswork, hopium, wishful thinking, and herd mentality, against 10% actual, factual data.

In short, it'll be an *extremely* poor decision process.

Your goal should be to reach a point where *at least 50%* of your decision is fact-based.

There's a specific reason for this.

Without facts-supported independent choice, you'll end up chasing rumor and hearsay, like everybody else. If you're in the majority, then you're too late - the real gains have already happened.

There's a very high chance you're buying high in hope, or selling low in panic.

That's how you *lose* money.

How to pick the right stocks is a science + art that can get very complex, deep, and involved... and while I definitely recommend learning this, if you're going to be seriously considering investing for the long term, it's too big a topic to squeeze in here.

• • •

But, there are some basics to start with.

- Understand the company you are planning to invest in.
- Is the company doing well already - i.e. low costs, high sales revenue, profits?
- Does it owe large debts, where paying them off will consume profits?
- Is the industry itself growing (or likely to grow in future)?
- Is it in an established, doing-well category?
- Are the products good, the management competent? No scams?
- Is your information coming from a reliable, competent source?

• • •

Time in market, beats timing the market.

Nobody can exactly predict when the exact low or high point of a stock will be, but the longer you keep doing it with a clear strategy, the better your chances of turning a profit. Don't chase quick returns. Expect to be slow.

Do not be emotional.

Do *not* buy or sell basis your own favorites, past experience, or feeling of loyalty. Define your rules, invest according to them, and then over time, keep improving the rules.

Sometimes these rules *will* lead to a loss; and that's ok.

Take the loss, but *understand why the rule failed.*

Fix it. Keep going.

• • •

Don't panic.

What goes up must come down, and vice versa, (unless you're going for the *completely* unknown companies, where just about *anything* can happen). You don't actually realize (make real) a loss until you actually *sell*, and nothing is a profit unless you cash out.

Sometimes you just have to be patient. A lot of dips are driven by rumor, fake news, or genuine (but temporary) cycles. Learn to ride them out.

● ● ●

Buy the dips.

Be contrarian: Buy when everyone is selling, sell when everyone is buying.

Majority of people lose 'playing' in stock markets, because of inexperience. They *panic* for the wrong reasons, or get too *greedy*. That's when volatility happens.

If you have a strategy in place, you can sell high in the upturn, or buy cheap on the downside.

You don't have to be the smartest person in the market... but if you can be smarter than just 51% of everyone else, you win.

● ● ●

Do not invest more than you are comfortable losing (or keeping frozen).

If the money you invested today remains stuck for weeks, months, even years in a major economic downturn, you should still be able to still put food on the table, and pay your bills. That's why you budget, keep RDs and FDs, have emergency funds.

Do *not* expect the stock market to obey *your* expectations and wishes, and follow *your* schedule.

Do *not* block money in the market that you need for something else, something important.

● ● ●

Never *ever* borrow to invest.

A huge mistake that happens when you get caught up in your emotions.

Something looks like a once-in-a-lifetime opportunity, a chance to change your entire future in one shot. You don't have enough to invest, so you take a loan to cover it.

One, the interest charges will eat away the profits, even if you're right.

Two, if you're wrong, you're well and truly screwed, because now you have an expensive debt to pay... and nothing to show for it.

And yes, using leverage tools is also borrowing to invest. Don't.

Not yet.

• • •

If something looks too good to be true, it usually is.

This is more generic advice that applies to most things; the surest sign of a scam is -

- a *short time period* to take action,
- *limited or nonexistent information,*
- a *single person* making things happen, and
- a beautiful - but *unsubstantiated* - vision of the future.

If you think you can turn your life around tomorrow because of a hot tip if you act now... it's a disaster that you just haven't seen yet.

• • •

Investing Styles

There's a couple of ways people invest.

- **Long term investing** - where you're in for over 3 years. You're buying shares keeping a long-term vision in mind, giving the company a chance to do well, based on the quality of their products and strategies, potential of their industry, growth of the economy, and a bunch of other factors. This approach has a decent chance of success, but needs careful research and patience.
- **Short term investing** - a window of a few days to months - where you see a quick opportunity based on changes in regulations, environment, economic trends, business cycles, or seasonality, and make a call on how rapidly this will impact the growth and profitability of the company. Higher risk, because you can be wrong, and things don't always work out the way you planned. Needs lots of experience and technical skills, awareness.
- **Day trading** - ultra short, i.e. within the same day. This one is highly speculative, and based completely on how the news of the day impacts

the way the general public feels. The % change (up or down) will be relatively low, so you'll need to put in large amounts of money to see a decent return. This also means if you're wrong, you stand to lose a lot of money, very fast.

Don' day-trade unless you're an expert. You're paying higher taxes, and running a very high risk of getting caught up in the emotional reactions, and making potentially very expensive mistakes.

No. 3 is very seductive, because you see immediate rewards if you're right. (At least a few times, initially.) But it comes with *very* high risk, because it is - or often becomes - an *emotional* choice, not rational.

If you're losing money, it can be hard to walk away from a bad trade, because walking away means admitting defeat. That's why people tend to keep chasing that bet, and end up losing a lot worse than they planned. They don't want to admit to failure.

And nobody ever talks about their failures. So you only hear about the successes.

It's also the one where you'll get maximum advice, social network scams, and peer-group 'inputs'.

Do *not* listen to these.

And for the love of God, stay off the hot tips and the Whatsapp / Telegram groups.

In the short term, the stock market is a *zero-sum game*; which means, for one person to win, *someone else has to lose*. The guy that can make other people do something - say, buy or sell X - has control over their actions, so he can make them lose - and himself win.

At the small scale, he might be charging fees for unverified tips; on the grand scale, he's manipulating the market.

Either way, you're putting your life and money in someone else's hands, and that's not investing.

Start with 1 - the *Long Term approach*. Get a feel of how the system works, pick relatively 'safer' bets, in large, known companies. You'll tend to be safer, and gain experience with lower risk.

For many people, this can be *all* they need to do, their whole lives, and *still* get a decent return beating the returns from savings accounts, FDs, inflation, mutual funds, and maybe even the market average. But it'll need patience, and controlling their panicky emotional decisions.

Move up to 2 - *Short Term* - once you have researched / studied enough to start making informed decisions, and test the quality of your decisions, with how much you burn your fingers.

You will lose multiple times here - but make sure you understand *why* you lost, and use that to make the next one better.

This is experimental, a way to test your knowledge and skill, and not the main investing strategy at this stage. It's all about being able to *control your panic*.

Keep 3 - Day Trading - for fun, and occasional bets, only well after you understand how everything works. It's gambling, and you should treat it as such - the occasional thrill, but not your long term plan.

And be okay with losing *everything* you invest, here. It'll happen more often than you think.

• • •

Risk

Risk is a critical thing to understand when you're playing around with equities.

One, do not give your money blindly to anyone with the expectation of some X return in Y time.

You'll meet plenty of people who'll give you an offer - *"My cousin quit his job and now trades fulltime. Give him 5L and he will 5X it in 3 years." "I can manage your wealth at my firm." "I started a portfolio management fintech startup." "Sir there is a special offer for our most valuable clients for unlisted securities."*

Stop. If you don't understand what they're doing, and have no control over how they use your money, then you're putting yourself in a dangerous place. Even apart from the risk of scams, the best-intentioned, trustworthy people can also make mistakes, or run into unexpected, Black-Swan events that wreck their investing strategy.

Or, they could get run over by a bus crossing the road tomorrow. What happens to your money then?

Your money, your control. If you want to invest, then learn to invest yourself.

Take ownership.

Two, understand that different sectors, and the economy itself, moves in large *cycles*.

This can depend on geopolitics, your own country's policies, the climate, the global economy. If something's been doing well the last few years, that doesn't guarantee it will continue to do so, in a straight line; understand why it's been doing well.

When a bunch of negative large-scale trends line up *together*, the overall market can fall dramatically, and stay down for a while.

That also means every Rs.100 you put in, may now be worth Rs. 50 or less. Do you have the resources, the ability (and the guts) to wait for a recovery? If too much of your money is parked in equity, you could wind up in a situation where it's worth much less at the time you really need it. (*Again, this is why you need an emergency fund!*)

Don't be forced to sell at a loss, against your will, because you invested money you needed for something else. It's only once you sell, that the loss becomes real.

Three, understand and build *diversification*.

Have a portfolio of a variety of investments, across size and sector.

Size - companies fall into three types:

- **Large-cap** - large, established companies with a high market cap, either with a large share volume and/or whose shares are worth a high amount. These will be slow to change and grow, but also slow to fall; They have access to deeper pockets, better resources, and higher expertise than others, so chances of failure in bad times is low.
  Unlikely to be impacted by anything less than **large-scale, long-term global events.**
- **Mid-cap** - medium-sized, upcoming companies. Tend to be lower-ranked than a largecap, but usually in established sectors.
  Because they're relatively small, they have a better chance of growing more in time, but also risk losing greater value if they fail.
- **Small-cap** - low value, highest risk. Finding the right one could give you a return in the multiples - 10x, 20x, 100x of your original investment - but equal (usually greater) possibility of seeing it all go to complete zero, as these are the companies in very early stages of their life with minimal resources, and therefore the most likely to fail in any bad circumstances.
  Smallcap values can be impacted by **small events** - rumor, regulation, scams, daily news, memes, etc. That's what makes it a bet - too many factors play into their daily performance, to be able to calculate accurately.

Diversifying across company sizes allows you to protect some monies in stable, large companies, while also giving an opportunity to put some into riskier areas that could give better growth. This way if a risk doesn't work out, you don't lose everything.

• • •

ector is the industry in which a company operates, like Banking, Auto, FMCG, IT, etc.

The reason we need to diversify across sectors, is because different sectors, are hit differently by different factors. For instance - good weather spells a good performance for agriculture, meaning rural regions have more money, so FMCG & Consumption does well. Good global economic conditions and trade, good for IT and shipping. A strong growing economy is good for infrastructure, power and construction, etc.

They all do well under certain circumstances, and badly under others - but these circumstances are all at different *times*. If you've got a decently balanced portfolio across sectors, *some* will always be up while others are down. This keeps the *average* up, and insulates the overall portfolio from large sudden shocks.

Research and identify what sectors can be the right ones to invest (more) in, compared to others, at a particular time. Balance out accordingly. Set your time horizon basis this.

The goal should be to get more invested in the sectors that will do well in the next few years, and when the balance starts to shift to others, adjust your investing accordingly.

Diversifying across sectors gives you the *opportunity to cash out parts of your portfolio at different times*, if that sector has done well, instead of being forced to liquidate something at a loss at the wrong time.

• • •

The Process: Getting started and continuing to invest

1. Open a demat account. Your bank's online portal will usually offer this, or you can go for a dedicated investment firm. Do your KYC, link your bank.
2. Add some money.
3. Select some stocks, buy.
4. Set a target date and value to sell, basis your research.

5. Track over time. Sell some. Get familiar with the process.
6. Then start building up a planned portfolio.

Set a periodic goal of investing an affordable, post-budget X amount - weekly, monthly, quarterly - and stick to that. This will help minimize emotional swings where you put too much too soon out of greed, and miss other better opportunities.

But, keep a '**dry powder**' amount aside as well each time - a small amount of money blocked for investing, but not actually invested yet. (*If you have a separate spare bank account, use that.*) Let this build over time, and have a *defined rule* (not an emotional judgment call) for *when* this can be used - eg. only if the market falls by over 10%.

This will happen rarely, but when it does, you'll have a very decent reserve of money to put in. This is for those once-in-a-year opportunities.

Needless to say, *stick to the blue-chip good quality stocks* in these disaster scenarios, because when the entire market is suffering that badly, there's a good chance that smaller companies will sink and go bankrupt, their stock value going to zero and taking all your hard-earned investment with it.

Set a rule for **exit**, i.e. sell out, as well. This means, for every company you buy, have a *target value* to be reached, and *target date*. If the target is met early, or missed on the target date, re-evaluate if you should exit anyway, or hang in there. Update a new set of targets.

Avoid building a very huge portfolio of hundreds and thousands of companies. It'll be hard to track, cumbersome to maintain - and will take much more effort per every buy or sell decision. Instead, try to limit to a few (under 5) select companies per sector, ideally across large and mid cap, with smallcap optional.

• • •

To Do

- Create a **portfolio structure** - no *actual* stocks yet, just a list, divided across mcap size, sector, and planned investment amount. The mcap split should be around 50-30-20, and the sector split can be as per your preference, research, gut feel, or vision.
- In each cell, list max 3 stocks. This becomes your selection portfolio.
- Include 2 targets - when will you *sell,* at profit, and at loss. These aren't simple numbers - they'll need a *lot* of thought, and work. But they're necessary to avoid a huge, unwieldy and unmanageable portfolio that you can't control, and have no strategy for handling.

Sector	Largecap	Midcap	Smallcap	Total
IT	Company 1 Company 2 Company 3	Company 4 Company 5	Company 6	(Sum of 1-6): keep < 20% of Grand Total
Banking	7, 8, 9	10, 11	12	< 20%
Auto	13, 14, 15	16, 17	18	< 20%
Etc etc	19, 20, 21	22, 23	24	
Total	(50% of Grand Total)	(30% of Grand Total)	(20% of Grand Total)	(Grand Total)

Following this guideline ensures you maintain a **broad diversification, limit investing** to a smaller set of companies (*or at least have a clear justification for why more are needed*), and **manage risk** by weighing greater amounts in safer, more reliable options, while remaining open to some high-risk, high return ones.

- Pick and choose what to buy / sell each month basis state of the market, keeping an eye on overall allocation so you don't break the diversification and risk management structure.

• • •

CHAPTER XXXIX

IPOs

A brief note - IPOs are, at least at this stage for you, a **high-risk proposition**. That's because -

- Companies launching IPOs *don't* have long-term track records, audited historical financials, and much of the data is hidden, or unreliable.
- They *do* have a major **hype cycle**, playing off general market sentiment and brand name recognition. Most IPOs happen during boom cycles, because money is available, and that's also when most people are feeling confident and optimistic.
- Every IPO launch spins up a powerful **PR engine** in the lead-up, circulating positive news, stories, building SEO, engaging influencers, seeding content. This creates a level of **positive buzz** very unlike the news-as-usual experienced by older listed companies; so for you, as a retail investor, it can be hard to disengage, discriminate between the two, and resist being influenced.
- Successes are highly visible, and there's **a strong element of FOMO.** There will be canteen and chai-tapri conversations with complete strangers about how much they made last time, how great this one is going to be... and after a while, given the lack of verifiable data, it becomes very hard to understand what's fact, and what's wishful thinking.
- Because IPOs can only be subscribed to in **specific lot sizes**, the lump-sum investment for any IPO can be significantly higher for a casual, early-stage investor than investing in listed shares.

Moral of the story - you cannot easily make objective, calculated, data-based decisions at the same level as regular equity investing.

So should you not do IPOs at all?

Here's an experiment. You give yourself a **limit** - you are going to invest in IPOs using the money you set aside for monthly equity investing, a maximum of two times in the first year. If both were successful, double it the second year. That's it.

This will force you to actually think hard about which IPO you want to go for, how to choose between them, and do as much actual research work as you can.

And if you make a bad choice once, twice... you get time to retreat, lick your wounds, and try again without ruining yourself. And think about where you messed up. It gives a close, personal experience of the hype that makes it easier to recognize the next time.

Of course, you could FOMO in and get lucky. Once, twice... maybe thrice. Then you'll get burned, and start over. That's fine - you're making a bet, and having fun. Enjoy it.

Just make sure it stays at the level of fun - no using money allocated for something else, no borrowing. If the first few bets pay off, use that as your next IPO bet fund.

• • •

CHAPTER XL

Intermission 5

"Kishore, you bastard, what have you done?!"

Sunil felt sick, physically nauseous. He he'd been glued to his phone, watching his stocks for the last three days continuously, wishing, hoping, and finally, desperately praying, for some change in direction.

No such luck. Prices kept going, giving an occasional mocking wiggle here and there, but down in a steady, deadly slide as inevitable as gravity.

Kishore had been avoiding him, and his calls and messages, ever since the day the IPO listed. All his confident, brash, and just-trust-me demeanor suddenly evaporated.

He'd finally caught him in the canteen, and cornered him before he could make some excuse and run off, and at last, here was his chance to get some answers.

"You said this was easy money! It was going to double, triple on listing! It was the hottest one of the year, everyone was waiting for this, so what the hell is happening?! Why's it not up, man? What's happening to my money?!!"

Kishore grimaced shamefacedly, avoiding his eyes. "Don't know, bhai. This guy who does my investing said-"

"What guy? You're the guy! You're supposed to be the expert! Now suddenly there's some guy?! I don't give a shit about any guy, you - you, Kishore - you promised me, now you get my money back!"

Kishore looked shifty, then went carefully blank-faced. He looked around, trying to spot if anyone was watching or listening.

"Sunil bhai, what are you saying? I never took any money from you. You only put it for the IPO. I just said this could be a -"

"Could be? Abe, you told me I will never get this chance again, I will be set for years! I put my full bonus on this! I-" Sunil also lowered his voice to a whisper, anger now mixed with shame at his own idiocy welling up.

"I took a- a loan out for this! I need the money!"

"I never told you to do all this, bhai," Kishore began sidling cautiously to one side. The canteen was mostly empty, but some people were now beginning to look their way, intrigued by the obvious tension. "Don't worry, this is just for now. It will go up for sure in a few months-"

"MONTHS!" yelled Sunil, completely forgetting himself and grabbing Kishore's collar. He felt his heart literally skip a beat, then start hammering double-time. Sweat beaded his forehead, a little fleck of spit flew from his mouth.

"I don't HAVE months to wait, saale-"

"Excuse me, is everything ok, Sunil?"

They both froze, Sunil's hand jumping back as if stung. Sakshi, his department VP, had walked up and was standing a few feet away, coffee in hand, wearing a questioning frown. Despite her height and normally a loud, dramatically-carrying voice, this time she'd come close in nearly ghost-like silence.

"Ji, madam," Kishore piped up immediately, stepping aside and adjusting his glasses. "Sunil bhai was just telling about the market, madam,"

"Hm. Well, don't waste time with all this during office, Sunil," she shook her head. "You have enough on your plate already, please focus."

"Y-yes, ma'am," Sunil choked down his rage, shaking. "I'm sorry, I- I have a meeting -"

"Yes, please carry on," she dismissed him, turning away. Kishore was already scuttling quickly down the passage, and Sunil knew he wouldn't be careless enough to be caught again - and so what if he was?

'He's right,' thought Sunil. 'He's actually not done anything wrong - he's just a fool talking out of his ass about things he didn't know anything about...'

'...and I was the bigger idiot, listening to him.'

He walked back to his desk, breathing deeply, anger sliding to a bleak, black depression.

He started mentally throwing away things, one by one, off his sinking life, somehow trying to pull together enough cash for the loan. The Diwali holiday... it was early, he could get an 80% refund from the hotel and flights. Definitely no car this year as planned, and no major shopping. Birthday cancel - actually, all parties cancel.

His wife would be furious, of course - he'd just have to put up with it for some time.

Maybe stay back late in office a few days a week, hopefully she'd be gone to sleep when he got home...

CHAPTER XLI

Other equity instruments – ETFs, REITs, Smallcases

Buying stocks directly gives great control over exactly *what* you're investing in, *when* to buy or sell, and grasp over the exact *composition* of your portfolio. However, every stock is a share in a specific company, which means you'll also need to know how to analyze and evaluate all those companies, keep actively tracking your stock portfolio, and the news, making continuous calls on buying or selling. It's *very* high-involvement; you can't afford to be out of date, or out of reach, for too long.

If you don't have the time, interest, or mindset for it, it can be a *massive* headache.

There are some instruments that offer a middle path, like **smallcases, ETFs, and REITs.** These, a little like mutual funds, consist of a group of stocks, focused around a sector, theme, categorization, or objective, but unlike the SIP-based MFs, can be quickly and easily bought and sold like stocks in the market.

• • •

ETFs and Smallcases are theme-based, objective-based, or strategy-based, available on exchanges and trading platforms. Another advantage of these, is that some stocks, especially for an early-stage investor, may tick all the boxes, but are simply too expensive individually to buy easily; and unlike the US, in India you can't buy fractional (part of) stocks.

An ETF-based approach allows you to focus on sectors and themes, without getting into individual stocks, and get exposure across different companies, without locking up too much capital in big, unwieldy chunks. You get the exposure of a MF, with the flexibility of an equity stock. It's a decent way to diversify your portfolio quickly, but also keep some control over entry/exit and rebalancing as well.

• • •

REITs are a slightly different animal. While different from stocks, ETFs, and MFs, they nevertheless are available in the same exchanges, and are bought and sold through the same process, so I'm including them here.

REITs are specific to real estate, usually commercial. Now, if you normally had to invest in real estate, it's a huge task, both in effort and money (and risk!) You'd have to identify a property for sale, evaluate returns, future growth, get the money together to buy it, manage it, collect rents, do maintenance, and everything else that comes with property ownership.

And this is not just any property, but a large-scale commercial property - an office building, hotel, industrial complex, warehouse, etc.

For someone in the first few years of working, this is pretty much *impossible*. Even if you win at KBC and get a couple of crores, it's not recommended - it takes a unique and deep skillset, and experience, to execute - and you would simply not have it at this time.

It's a full-time job for an entire company. You *cannot* do it part-time.

However, REITs (*Real Estate Investment Trusts*) *are* that full-time company. They do the research and evaluation, handle the purchase, collection, maintenance, and sale, and pay you a share of the rents they collect as dividends.

All you have to do, is invest small amounts regularly, by buying the REIT stocks. It's like a MF for real estate. This way you get ownership into real estate as an investment category, without a lot of the risk and high capital investment.

These 3 options, they're are smaller steps into higher-risk, higher-return investing, where you take part in the market, and beat inflation, without having to become an expert, full-time stock analyst (*though it helps!*), and offer you a chance to diversify your investing without having to lock up huge amounts in illiquid instruments.

• • •

To Do

Not much at this stage - just -

- Learn what are ETFs, Smallcases, REITs and how they work
- Identify platforms and processes for purchase
- Identify top 2-3 options in each, matching your overall investment strategy
- This includes top 2-3 choices of specific funds or instruments in each sector as well.
- Plan a gradual investment process - X amount, distributed across these categories, for a few months to a year.
- End of the year, evaluate the performance and returns. Don't be in a rush. Compare to the overall market, similar instruments. Decide if you want to modify or continue.
- Each year, re-jig your focus in sectors and themes basis the news and expected future growth. It's complicated, but following it will be an invaluable experience in learning about macro factors and how the overall economy plays a role in the cyclical rise and fall of specific sectors.

• • •

CHAPTER XLII

Other Investing Options

I've talked about maximizing income, clearing debt, saving money, covering for emergencies, and finally, **basic investing.** Beyond FDs, PPFs and similar retirement plan instruments, mutual funds and equities are some of the standard, higher-return early investment vehicles to start with in the initial years, establishing a strong base of knowledge, habit, and expertise on which you can build others.

Now, as you move ahead, *more* options for investing become available. These are more complex, require greater upfront capital or a different timescale, and carry their own unique systems, risks and knowledge requirements.

In short - you'll find there'll be **no end to where you can put your money.** What you *will* need to have in place, though, is **a cognitive framework** - structured mental model for evaluating options, a disciplined approach, and a checklist for how you approach them.

1. Do you have more *money* to invest, without damaging or risking other goals?
   If you control spending and bad debt, avoid major mistakes, and are doing even reasonably ok at work, 1-2 promotions or job shifts will very quickly make this available.
2. Can you *learn* about these new opportunities, and how to invest in them, to a level where you can be competent? Or does it require you to acquire a skillset or put in time that you simply don't have?
3. Can you objectively *judge* between different options, and understand which are better than others?
4. Do you have the *mental bandwidth,* i.e. simply enough time to think - to juggle all your investments and financial products?
5. Do you have an *exit strategy* - a clear understanding of what you can expect out of each investment, and be able to evaluate if it's working or not, so you can get out in time?
6. What's the *opportunity cost* - would you be better off expanding what you already know and do, rather than get into something new?

These are *hard* questions to answer, and maybe you won't have all the answers at first. It's ok to test and fail - as long as the experiment used money and time you could afford to lose, and you walked away with some idea of either how to succeed, or why you failed.

If you got nothing - maybe that particular opportunity wasn't right for you at this time.

But if you *do* have the answers in place, then selecting and handling additional investments in future becomes - maybe easier, but at least more manageable and profitable, or less likely to wreck you.

Some other popular options for parking your cash -

• • •

A is for All That Glitters

Gold & Silver (and platinum, diamonds, gems, and more.)

The old favorite, possibly one of the very earliest ways in which people saved. It's actually not a bad option - reasonably liquid, usually keeps up with inflation, and is a traditionally acceptable instrument. You can buy this as either physical metal, jewelry, digital, or sovereign bonds.

- **Physical Gold / Silver,** coins or bars, or **Gems.** Sold and bought by most jewelry retailers, easy to store. Make sure you work with reliable partners, and have a safe place to store it. There will be moderate making charges involved.
  Risk: Your biggest risk really is getting scammed with **poor quality or fake products**, or having it physically stolen.
- **Jewelry** - like physical, but making charges are higher due to greater complexity. Equal risk of theft, fraud or other loss. But has a major advantage in having utility - it can be worn and/or gifted. The intangible social benefits come free, over & above a simple value calculation, and *can* play a bigger part in **general happiness** than you think.
- **Gold schemes** - offered as an investment instrument by retailers, works like a SIP until you have enough accumulated to buy physical gold. Getting slightly into hybrid territory here - are you better off doing a SIP yourself, and just buying gold with the proceeds?
  Risk: Does a jewellery retailer have the expertise to handle investments for you?
- **Digital gold** - offered as an investment instrument by fintech corporations. Are backed by physical gold held, easy to buy / sell, flexible timings, market-driven prices, no risk of self-custody.
  Risk: Where are you buying it from? Remember, it's all digital - you never actually get it in your hands. Very high scam potential if buying from unknown or less-than-reliable sources.
- **Sovereign gold bonds (SGBs)** - these are also virtually held, issued by selected banks at appointed release times, and backed by a government guarantee. All the value & appreciation, no making charges, and offer some benefits in terms of interest earned and tax benefits. Have a minimum holding period.

• • •

B is for Bonds

Corporate Bonds, Government securities and T-bills.

The other side of the investing coin - these are **debt instruments.**

They're offered by corporations and the government periodically, and can be understood as the government or the corporate borrowing money from you, for an X duration, to fulfill some objective or project. In return, they reward you with a certain interest.

These tend to be **relatively safer**, as they are backed by very large entities that aren't likely to collapse or fail.

Pros -

- It's a comparatively **safer** place to park your money, and get (slightly) better returns compared to leaving it in a bank FD.
- Duration is variable, but can be relatively a much shorter term than an FD.

Cons -

- Not always available for purchase on demand
- Sometimes needs a comparatively higher investment amount compared to others, in some cases.

These have a different purpose. They aren't there to grow your money or give high returns.

They can be seen as good **money protectors.** There's no huge upside, but also **very little risk** or downside either; so once you've made some gains, parking those gains here, while you wait for the right time to re-enter the market, is a way to keep your profits safe.

Secondly, as you get closer towards **retirement**, start thinking about how to *protect* your earnings, rather than continuing to run the risk of direct market exposure that may fall in value when you need it. Your goal should now be moving to stability, security, and safety, not the adrenaline of dramatic outperformance.

Thumb rule: 100 - (your age) = % of your investments in relatively higher-risk instruments.

• • •

C is for Cryptocurrency

Tokens, Coins, NFTs, and more.

Yes, there's **utility** in crypto, an opportunity to solve existing real-world financial problems and use cases.

Yes, it's a highly **technical** product in an advanced, cutting-edge technology ecosystem.

Yes, it's **hard to understand** for most people, as the utility, process, and operations require some advanced technological expertise to understand.

Yes, some people have made **insane amounts of real money**, far greater than seasoned industry titans have made in generations, often with seemingly very little effort.

Add it all up... and, for a regular mango person, you get this mysterious, magical thing, that through means unknown, can take very little work and money - and turn it into **life-changing gains**.

It's better than the bag of stolen money dropped in your garden, better than finding buried treasure or an undiscovered Husain in your grandfather's trunk, better than winning the lottery...

But it's very new, with minimal history, and nearly *nobody* (at least in the in the general population) knows precisely how the hell it works.

So, anything and everything associated with it, is fair game for being seen as a pathway to easy, fast, cheap riches.

Do you hear how that sounds?

That's right.

There's no such thing as an easy, fast, and cheap path to success.

In crypto's case, what's missing is the 'easy' part. You need to learn what it is, how it works, and how to evaluate, save, and use it.

And that needs *very* high-level education, expertise and exposure to cutting-edge tech.

If you don't... scam city's waiting for you.

I'll keep this basic, because this is a very fast-evolving space, so any details I give will be obsolete by the time I end this sentence.

There's 2 ways you get into crypto -

1. As a **speculator** - where you are coming in with the pure expectation of seeing the value of the tokens you bought go up.
2. As a **utility user** - where you *understand and use* the utility offered by the token in the crypto ecosystem. Thousands of use cases exist.

In both cases, there are levels and categories of tokens available. There are blue-chip equivalents, mid-scale utilities, and small new tokens and memecoins with potential to flash into popularity.

Just remember **3 core things** -

1. It's a *highly technical product* and has its own rules of what makes it useful / valuable, so you need to have familiarity with the ecosystem in which any token operates; plus, familiarity with the way the token itself is built and distributed. Keep in mind this is advanced tech, so there will be high complexity.

2. It's like *stocks on speed*, i.e. much, much more volatile, with faster cycles and bigger swings. It's always-on; no limited trading hours, so you could be 90% wiped out in a matter of minutes while you're asleep. There's high regulatory risk, because it's so new; there are (mostly) no laws governing it, meaning new ones could come up anytime.

3. It's all *self-custody and decentralized*, so there's no authority to approach if you make a mistake and want to reverse it. You lose access, it's gone. You send to the wrong address, or in the wrong network, it's gone. If you keep it on a central exchange, and the exchange or bridge gets exploited, it's gone. The developer abandons the project and runs, it's gone.

However, that said - it's also **a very interesting opportunity to experiment with.** Worth parking a small amount, and putting in some time to learn, just to understand concepts and systems. Just assume you're going to lose it all, in exchange for knowledge gained, in the initial periods, and invest accordingly.

DYOR.

It's not easy, but it can be fun, useful, and beneficial.

If it looks fast, easy, and cheap... then you're already being scammed.

• • •

D is for Derivatives

Futures & Options.

You will hear a *lot* about these in the finance classrooms of Whatsapp University.

Myths and legends of that unknown (friend of a friend) person, who 10x'd his cash every day and turned a single rupee into a multi-crore mansion, in a matter of months if not weeks.

You'll hear a lot about how every second person has apparently quit his job to do this full-time, and gained amazing health, fantastical wealth, and lasting mental peace.

Let me try to describe what's wrong with this picture, **with a ridiculous example.**

See, a Formula One race car *can* go faster than a bicycle.

But that doesn't mean that everyone who's currently cycling, can suddenly hop behind the wheel of that F1 machine, and immediately expect the same results as a Lewis Hamilton.

(*Maybe a Senna, though.*

Sorry, that... was a very dark joke.

Moving on.)

These are *complex* and *sophisticated* financial instruments. They need detailed understanding and experience to use; and 99% of people *don't* have it.

And if you don't understand it, it's gambling. It literally gets described as a bet.

If you want to place bets, go to Goa, take a trip on the riverboat casinos. You'll lose the same money, but at least you got a nice holiday out of it.

Seriously. It ruins lives. Don't risk it without understanding it.
Get behind that wheel without knowing how to drive, and you will crash and burn horribly.

• • •

CHAPTER XLIII

Wealth Management Services and Wealth Managers

A little note about wealth managers and wealth management services.

Tread with caution.

Wealth Management as a service is fine, in fact actually important and necessary.

You just don't need it so *early*.

Wealth management typically comes into play, when you reach that level of riches that you need professional expertise to manage the entire gamut of your financial operations - taxation, wealth safeguarding, diversification, etc. etc., at scale.

You simply do not have the time, expertise or energy to do it yourself, at that level.

Your actual job or business is the one where your time should be invested, because that's what is bringing in the money. That's where your expertise lies. That's where you're better than anyone else.

There's an old joke that goes - *If Bill Gates dropped a $100 bill, he would leave it and keep walking, because the time he wastes bending down to pick it up, he would have made more money just continuing to do what he was doing before.*

Think of learning to manage large amounts of wealth - and all the expertise areas that involves, in finance and law, in people skills and technical expertise - learning to do all that will make you a wealth manager, not a person whose wealth needs managing.

Instead, focus on being that person (with the wealth). You already know how.

Second, Wealth management operates at *scale*, over a *long time horizon*. *You don't need it yet.*

Third, be aware that a lot of so-called 'wealth managers' are essentially **agents** selling a specific product, or limited basket of products. They make their money from the *sale*. *Your* long-term financial wealth, once they've made the sale, is irrelevant to them... just as long as you don't do so badly, that you come after them with a hockey stick.

They've already *made their commission.*

When all you have is a hammer, then everything looks like a nail.

If they have a single product at their disposal, then that single product becomes the answer to every problem you ask.

Want to grow your money? LIC policy. Safeguard your money? LIC policy. Annuity? LIC policy. Diversify risk? LIC policy. Insurance? Hmm, maybe LIC policy. Invest in cryptocurrency? That's risky, buy LIC policy instead.

And I know I'm mocking the LIC network, and apologies - but it's just to prove a point. LIC's actually a great product, within the scope of insurance.

The same behavior is true of anyone selling a specific ULIP, or mutual fund, teak farm, chit fund, land plot, meme coin, or NBFC product. It becomes the answer to *everything.*

Just be clear where the wealth manager is making his money from. Follow the money. Motivations will become clear immediately... and so will your understanding of exactly how relevant their advice is.

And lastly - your **CA**, or that one guy in accounts who helps out in filing your taxes on the side... he is *not* a wealth manager.

• • •

CHAPTER XLIV

Recap – Your Personal Finance Journey Checklist

Let's see how we're progressing through the journey, shall we? How many more of the list have we been able to check off so far?

I have -

- Decided to take control of my personal finances
- Allocated a dedicated storage area for my documentation
- Understood the basic concepts of inflation, compounding, and risk
- Made a monthly budget, and follow it
- Familiarized myself with my salary structure and all benefits
- Purchased life insurance with payout of at least a year's earning
- Purchased personal health insurance with all critical riders
- Set up an emergency fund of at least 3 months' income
- Automated standard bill payments
- Cleared all my outstanding credit card and high-interest debts
- Reduced regular debts to under 30% of income
- Started contributing to a functional retirement account
- Utilized fully the tax saver components of my salary
- Deployed goal-based RDs
- Saved in at least one long-term FD
- Created a diversified mutual fund portfolio
- Invested in a diversified equity portfolio
- Explored 1-2 alternative investments
- Secured my digital footprint and credentials
- Started researching alternative income streams
- Planned the regular biannual physical checkup
- Vacationed at least once a year
- Reviewed each of the above in detail every 5 years.

Digital Savvy

There is no patch for stupidity.

Kevin Mitnick

CHAPTER XLV

Good Digital Habits

You're doing well, if you've got to here - you've sorted out your work and life, handled the essentials, are keeping daily life running smoothly, and are saving & growing a decent amount of cash to make your future dreams come true.

This cash is mostly sitting in a bank, or brokerage, account. An account **accessible via website or app.** Linked to a **username, password, email, or mobile number** - which means, it's accessible to *anyone* who gets your credentials or phone.

The world's getting increasingly complex, and sophisticated tools are becoming available to malicious actors. Meanwhile, financial sites & apps, organisations, digital tools, and storage mechanisms are continuously growing and evolving, incorporating new tech, corporate acquisitions, and hiring personnel at breakneck speed to keep up with the pace of the world.

This creates a lot of gaps, vulnerabilities, and legally gray areas in the process.

The chances are, that when - not if - you are targeted in a scam, it *will* be sooner than later.

You need to develop good digital habits.

• • •

Guard your own data

You know why everyone asks for PII data, KYC, etc? So you're identifiable, your credit score can be referenced, and as you pay back loans, your creditworthiness is updated.

You know why bad agents want this same data? *Data - it's the new oil.*

Data can be bought and sold, passing through steadily less trustworthy and decreasingly reliable channels, leaking, getting copied, until it finds its way to an unscrupulous data broker or a darkweb site, available at a ridiculously low price, for whoever wants to buy it.

You know why these persons unknown buy (or steal, or otherwise acquire) that data?

It can be used to endlessly **spam** you. It can be used to build a profile to be used in both primitive and sophisticated **scams.** It can be used to create

fake identities and profiles, which can be used to take unauthorized loans and credit cards by criminals, leaving you to deal with repayment and the aftermath. It can be used, say, to buy a phone SIM card that gets used in communicating with a terrorist cell.

Your data is precious, and it's very dangerous in the wrong hands. Hang onto it, protect it, give it out only when necessary, only to reliable people. Once you've given it, it's **out of your hands** - so think twice, three times, before taking that pic of your Aadhar and sending it off on Whatsapp or some random chat / number, or handing over xeroxes to some random unknown delivery guy or agent.

The safest place to keep a true secret is in your own head.

The *least* safe place is in digital format, unencrypted, on a device that's connected to the internet... and then **talking about it.**

• • •

The 5-dollar wrench attack

Let's say you encrypt your passwords and account details, store them in a secured, updated computer with high-quality antivirus and antimalware packages, behind strong firewalls and advanced security tools, in a steel-door locked room.

This *may* stop a North Korea-backed hacker from remotely accessing and stealing your data. It will be absolutely *useless* against 2 guys grabbing you in an alley, and beating you with an iron rod until you hand it over.

Don't talk about how much money you have, and don't show it off.

You're asking for trouble.

• • •

Safeguard your Personal Devices

- **Use good passwords.** Don't write them on post-its, and stick them to your monitor. Don't use 'abc123'. Don't use the same password for everything. Yes, it's hard work. But a critical skill.
- Learn to use a password manager.
- If you *have* to share or use a personal password on a public, or someone else's device, **change it fast**, as soon as you can. You don't control their security measures or past / future actions.
- Put **MFA** on financial websites, and on those email accounts where verification requests come. Use **separate email accounts** for bank /

money transaction site logins vs regular personal emails.

Don't give me that look - you know your phone can support effectively unlimited email IDs.

- Set **limits** for online transactions, UPI payments, atm withdrawals, and credit cards.
- Use a **separate, low-limit credit card** for online transactions and subscriptions.
- Set **alerts** for unusual activity, especially withdrawals or beneficiary additions.
- Never click on an **unknown link** in an email, or sms, or whatsapp. When in doubt, go to the corporate website and verify.
- Install an **antivirus** on your laptop, computer, tablet, and phone. A good, *paid* one, not freeware.
- Keep unlock **authentication** on your phone, preferably biometric or complex-pattern. Not a '0000' passcode.
- If you *must* have an NFC-based payment system on your phone, link it to a low-value card.
- **Learn** how to locate, block, and remotely wipe & brick your phone, if it gets lost or stolen.

• • •

Track Access, Emergencies, and Documentation

- Lookup and keep the key bank and brokerage **helpline** and **Relationship Manager numbers** saved. Check if there are any working hours or time restrictions.
- Know how and where to report cybercrime, fraud, etc. Locations, sites, phone numbers.
- **Make a will.** It's not morbid or "inviting misfortune"; it just ensures your descendants (for whom you're doing all this anyway) don't get cheated out of their dues, or forced to run through administrative / legal loops.
- Use **cold storage** where relevant.
- List your assets, investments, accounts, properties, and instructions, and keep in a **safe deposit locker.** Ensure at least 2-3 trusted people are aware of this.
- Keep critical original documents saved as scans on a secure location, separate from your physical residence. A USB drive in that same locker

is a good idea.

- Do not hand out PII data to anyone who asks. Everyone's hungry for your data, and there are algorithms building a complex map of who you are, with every major organization. Most of the time, it gets leaked.
- Have a verbal password, agreed upon with close family and friends, in case of emergency money transfer requests. AI tools can perfectly simulate anyone's voice with 5 seconds of audio. Very soon they'll be able to use video too.

• • •

Scam Self-Education

- **Read up** about how common scams happen.
- Know where your funds are, how to access and monitor them, and how to **freeze** them in an emergency.
- Most of all, learn how to recognize the common signs of a scam email or sms - misspelled website names and extensions, mismatched email addresses, poor English, and **the most critical tell-tale signs.** It's a scam if they -

  - Are asking you to do something to avoid harm or prosecution, **right now.**
  - Are offering something for free - Nigerian gold, a fully-paid-up holiday, *'fraandship'*, a job, a role, emigration, even a basic package delivery.
  - Claim to have something of yours that you didn't order.

• • •

Tracking your CIBIL score

Keep an eye on your CIBIL score.

As you build good investing and financial habits, your credit score will begin to reflect the same. Maintaining a good credit score can be very useful in the future, when you have to apply for loans, get approvals, or qualify for certain positions.

A credit score also lets you track your **financial identity**, and can act as an **early-warning system** for potential fraud or identity theft. If your personal data was leaked, and someone is attempting to misuse it - take out loans, credit checks,etc - *immediately* have it reported. It might be inconvenient, and involve some legwork and admin work, but getting stuck in a fraud case can become a nightmare later - loan issues, visa approvals, international travel, tax implications, all start getting affected.

Not to mention random harassment from mistaken credit recovery agents.

• • •

Setup online payments

Get familiar with **online payments, ECS, SIPs, and autopay.**

The technology exists today to make life *much* simpler; the goal of using it is not just to avoid standing in lines and wasting time, but also to not accidentally *forget* to pay something, and incur both penalty charges, as well as interrupted service and mental stress.

It's also a protection. If you know how online payments work, you're less likely to get fooled into making a fake transaction on an unfamiliar site in the heat of the moment.

- The standard payments for **utility bills** should be set on autopay.
- **Subscriptions** (especially online) can also be set to autopay from a credit card.
- **Payments in cash** - domestic help salaries, small jobs, services for the month - should be allocated into a set place, a specific drawer or envelope, from where cash can be handed out.
- SIPs, EMIs, and regular small-to-moderate payments (eg. insurance, recharges) should be automated on **ECS.**
- Large irregular payments (like credit card bills) should be paid **online, but manually.** Try and do this payment as soon as the bill generates, rather than waiting for the last day. I'm recommending *not* making this automatic, to make sure the payment is a conscious decision based on an awareness of available funds. Don't risk an extra-large bill draining your account making an EMI fail.
- If you have a fixed amount for **money transfer** - savings, rent, sending money home for parents, etc that you know how much and when, set it up as a recurring payment on a fixed date.
- **Don't** schedule every auto payment within the 1st 4 days of the month - there can be public or bank holidays, inconveniently timed weekends, or

salary delays. Ensure you have the money before paying out.

- Keep a track of the dates when payments happen, so you can ensure there's enough balance for the payments.

• • •

CHAPTER XLVI

The Regular Review

What - you thought if you got till here, you're *done?*

By reaching till here, you expected that you've become some kind of personal finance expert, master of your fate and captain of your soul, completely on-board and up-to-date on all aspects of your money and your life, ready to tackle anything that life throws at you and all set for riches untold?

Ha. Ha. Ha.

If you *have* got till this point, you've taken (*or should have taken*) at least a year, probably two, to get everything sorted.

If less, I'm afraid there's likely to be a nasty surprise waiting for you around the next corner - be warned.

It's been hard work, tiring, and has involved a lot of prep, piles of documentation, weeks of organizing, a fuckton of research, learning, and education, and finally, at least one good night's sleep.

Time has passed.

And the world has moved on.

You're promoted, now earning more.

Possibly engaged, married, parented. Dependents an expenses have increased, time has not.

A bank's collapsed, the economy's evolved, a government's changed and brought new policies, rules, and issued random bans.

Some dictator, or politician somewhere, has declared a hot, cold, or trade war. Trade has taken a hit, FIIs have withdrawn. Inflation and interest rates have changed.

You've taken on more debt, bought a house, won a lottery, or made some bad decisions.

A lot of people, companies and services have hiked their fees.

A new financial product has revolutionized or upended the financial world.

In short - everything is different.

And so are the **drivers of your personal finance plan**, which means your plan is likely *already* obsolete in some critical areas, and now has a good chance of going off the rails, left unchecked.

So first of all, you need to *revisit your goals.*

Then, you need to revisit *every aspect* of the personal finance plan aligned with those goals - your insured amounts, your emergency fund size, your documents, nominees, investment spread, diversification splits, choice of investments.

See if each one still aligns to the new world and the new goals. If not, see what needs to be changed.

This is a big exercise, and should be approached in the spirit of a clean slate - imagine you are sitting down to make this plan for the first time.

But what's different of who you now are, and what you're bringing to the table. What you bring to the exercise, is the knowledge & expertise gained in the last few years, the assets earned.

And before you panic -

You *don't* need to do this too often.

For instance, try limiting this activity to the start of all years ending with 0 or 5.

• • •

Recap: Your Personal Finance Journey Checklist

Let's see how we're progressing through the journey, shall we? How many more of the list have we been able to check off so far?

I have -

- Decided to take control of my personal finances
- Allocated a dedicated storage area for my documentation
- Understood the basic concepts of inflation, compounding, and risk
- Made a monthly budget, and follow it
- Familiarized myself with my salary structure and all benefits
- Purchased life insurance with payout of at least a year's earning
- Purchased personal health insurance with all critical riders
- Set up an emergency fund of at least 3 months' income
- Automated standard bill payments
- Cleared all my outstanding credit card and high-interest debts
- Reduced regular debts to under 30% of income
- Started contributing to a functional retirement account
- Utilized fully the tax saver components of my salary
- Deployed goal-based RDs
- Saved in at least one long-term FD
- Created a diversified mutual fund portfolio
- Invested in a diversified equity portfolio
- Explored 1-2 alternative investments
- Secured my digital footprint and credentials
- Started researching alternative income streams
- Planned the regular biannual physical checkup
- Vacationed at least once a year
- Reviewed each of the above in detail every 5 years.

FIRE

The ultimate purpose of money is so that you don't have to be in a specific place, at a specific time, doing anything you don't want to do.

Naval Ravikant

CHAPTER XLVIII

Secondary Income Streams

If you're in the **first couple of years** of your working life, you probably won't (or shouldn't) have time for establishing parallel income streams. But that doesn't mean, don't lay the *groundwork*.

At some time, hopefully, your actual career will have reached a place where it can be handled on autopilot, and you have time available to pursue a hobby. The foremost point of a hobby, is *mental peace, de-stressing and entertainment*; these should continue to be the primary justification. But some leisure activities can be monetizable as well.

This also isn't a suggestion that you *must* do something on the side; sometimes a career is all you need for managing your income, expenses and investing. But sometimes, **a side hustle** can be useful in supplementing a stagnant career, becoming a full-time passion project post-retirement - or maybe even becoming a path to an early retirement.

There will be thousands of options, but *not all are equal.*

- Some will be pointless time sinks, with little or no potential for growth, insignificant monies, or low satisfaction (*like the loss-making boutique on the ground floor*).
- Some will be *too complex, time- or effort-intensive*, to run easily.
- Some will *not be owned by you*, i.e. you'll be working to make money for someone else. Eg. Any kind of MLM, etc.
- And some, they'll be outright *scams* (*remember the teak or sandalwood estate schemes from back in the 90s?*).

Look for stuff that -

- You're already good at, or know about
- Lets you learn something new, that you enjoy;
- Can be done over weekends / an hour a day;
- Doesn't require any major cash investments;
- Builds a useful network;
- Has potential to scale up in future.

For example -

- **Teaching / speaking** about something you're already a core SME in, which eventually becomes focused consulting;
- **Content creation:** Writing a book, blog, social media, youtube or IG channel;
- **AirBNB:** If you have a property, explore how it can be used as an AirBNB type commercial vacation home, rather than just pure rental income;
- **Freelancing** with technical / creative skills

This is just an *indicative* list; there are many, *many* more. But always, look for something where you **own it yourself.**

Otherwise, you're just doing 2 jobs, and making 2 *other* people richer. While your own life and time becomes shorter.

• • •

To Do

The point of this, so early, is not to set up a parallel income stream (at least, not yet).

Instead, it's meant to start the *thinking process,* so you have some idea on how to build this in future.

- Start with your own *interests and skills.* What are you good at, enjoy doing - and more importantly, rule out what you're not enthused with. Not everyone is a natural entrepreneur, educator, content creator, etc. Just because someone else is doing it, doesn't mean you should, or even can.
- List what are some ways in which any money can be earned on the side. Try to make this a long, comprehensive list, and it'll keep growing over time as new opportunities emerge.
- Against each one, **assess and identify** -

  - what are the *skills and capabilities* needed, any specific qualifications or experience.
  - What is the *effort* involved? How much time will it take, for how long?
  - Are there any *legal or capital requirements*, or ongoing expenses?
  - Do you need to get any *specialist equipment, space, licenses, training, certifications?*
  - Is there a dependency on *access to specific groups* - either clients, audience, a network, mentors, gatekeepers, suppliers, contacts?

Now to stage two.

- How do you match up against this, today, and later? Do you see this evolving into something big?
- Does it match your interests and personality type, existing and planned work and education?
- Can you evolve to meet the requirements of an area you have an interest in?

The point is not to shut doors, or force you into a specific path; opportunities can come anytime, in any form. How well you utilize them, will depend on both natural inclinations, as well as basic preparedness.

Being aware of what you *need to succeed*, can shave off precious months, or years, from the process... and help pre-navigate some inevitable problems and obstacles, by being prepared instead of trial and error.

• • •

CHAPTER XLIX

Passive Income

The primary purpose of investing is to grow and safeguard your money, but it also has a *second* purpose - **passive income.**

This is what people mean when they say, '*make your money work for you.*' You've already been earning passive income the day you opened your first bank account... but with investing, you get some options to expand this.

Annuities (Pensions)

Once upon a time, you'd work for an employer as soon as you were qualified, till the day you retired, decades later. That benevolent, generous employer would reward your time and hard work, not only with a salary during employment, but also afterwards with a monthly pension.

So, you lived happily ever after.

If this sounds like a fairy tale... that's because it is.

Today, almost *no* private employers do this. Some (government jobs) do, but the amount of pension given has usually been calculated as per a 1950s lifestyle, and has *zero* bearing on modern reality, and current cost of living.

Therefore, ensuring that **Future You** (*old and decrepit, possibly senile, definitely unemployable*) still has a roof over his head, and food on his plate... that responsibility falls to **Current You.**

Remember that **NPS, EPF and PPF** we talked about way back? Now you're 60 years old, and have cashed out that PPF, taken 40% of that NPS.

Hopefully, you've been diligent about investing regularly, and it's a nice tidy sum.

You *could*, at this point, go berserk like you won the lottery, and burn through it all before the horrified eyes of your (*hopefully*) hard-working children, in a year-long orgy of **drink, debauchery** and **conspicuous consumption**, until you're once more penniless, and completely dependent on those very same, now inheritance-less, children to look after your ancient self till you die.

Or, you could put it into -

• • •

Annuities.

These are like a mirror image of mutual funds; instead of investing a little each month for a big payout at the end, you put a big chunk at the start, and get back a little each month. This should target replacing (*some, or most of,*) your salary income, and ensure you can still meet living expenses without dependency on anyone.

• • •

SWPs

Again, a very similar concept, a mirror-image to SIPs. If you have a big lump-sum available, and haven't thought of any specific, useful place to invest it, then put it in a MF and set a *Systematic Withdrawal Plan*. Set the duration and volume. The lump sum will grow like an invested mutual fund, but you keep taking out a little each month. If you aren't withdrawing so much that you drain the principal amount, this could keep going forever (*apart from the lost value due to inflation*).

And when you do finally ascend to the Great Beyond, there's still a nice chunk of change left over for your descendants. Love and filial responsibility is great for getting support in your old age, but a little pinch of greed makes it even more effective.

• • •

Dividend income

Those thousands and thousands of blue-chip company shares you picked up over the years? *You don't have to sell them.*

If those companies are paying out **dividends** - and most do, especially the blue-chip PSUs - then you should be having a small, but steady, income stream coming in, just for ownership of those shares. Remember, a 'share' means a 'share of profit' of that company.

This is a side effect - the primary purpose of buying and owning those shares, was to benefit from the appreciation in their value. But along the way, you can also benefit from the divided income they bring.

At first, it'll be laughably tiny, barely covering your bus fare to work. Then one day, it'll pay for lunch. Then the EMI on that flight ticket or new car... and finally, with discipline, brains, and a little luck, supplanting your salary income.

At that point, you'll have achieved the *dream* of every salaried person struggling through the toxic environment of a dysfunctional office under a psycho boss.

You'll have achieved fuck-you money.

Fuck-you money is the money that says - you no longer have to put up with toxic shit anymore, and you can walk away whenever you want.

It's where you can tell your boss, *"No, sorry sir, I will not come in on Saturday again, or ever put up with your bullshit ever again sir, so fuck off. Sir."*

(*actually, on second thoughts, don't do this, however tempting it sounds - while you can always leave, it's better to leave on a good note - you don't want to make enemies for no reason. The world is round - travel far enough and you will always meet the same people again.*)

But fuck-you money will give you the *best night's sleep you have ever had*, every night, knowing that you don't have to listen to anyone's bullshit out of desperation and fear, ever again.

If your parallel income can support all your needs, and most of your (reasonable) wants, you can actually stop working, catch a breath, and maybe focus on turning that hobby into a rewarding second career.

As long as, of course, you haven't let your *lifestyle* grow to a level where it's unsustainable without that horrible job. Remember that's a choice you made, every time you maxed out your credit card, or spent that extra few lakhs on something unnecessary or irrelevant. The choice to keep working a terrible job for a horrible boss, because you need that work to survive, and pay for your bad spending habits.

The more you control your lifestyle, the more you can invest, leading to faster time to FYM and more sustainable and realistic early retirement with financial independence.

Every gulab jamun you eat costs you 30 minutes next morning on the treadmill. Which is stronger - your love of gulab jamuns, or hatred of the treadmill?

• • •

CHAPTER L

Health

Talking of gulab jamuns, I should bring this up as well.

Watch your health.

No, I haven't suddenly lost track of what I'm doing, and started writing a health guide.

Staying in the context of what this book's all about, *not* taking care of your health will hand you a painful, chronic, debilitating, *expensive* disease or three, each of them a massive money drain in your post-retirement, as it all catches up with you at the time when your age is against you.

All the late nights, unhealthy snacks, coffee overdoses, pre- and post-meeting stress smoking, hours of sitting in bad chairs peering into screens... it's all been adding up like an **SIP of sickness**, and it has now matured.

Being sick when old means longer recoveries, more expensive treatments... so higher costs.

Plus, dropping dead of a work stress-linked heart attack at 46, can put a serious dent in your future earning ability.

Choose Ikigai over Karoshi.

On the other hand, obsessively counting steps, sleep hours, calories, fad diets, running time, intense workouts, intermittent fasting, and the works - That's also counterproductive.

You'll end up wrecking either your body, or your peace of mind, both of which put you in the same place - long expensive treatments and hospitalizations, with a real risk that you die.

Eat decent food, destress, do some physical activity, sleep properly.

That's all you need.

• • •

Mental Health

I'm no psychologist either, so I won't give out mental health advice. But I will suggest what's worked for me, in resolving issues that used to keep me worried.

- The goal of taking control of your finances is to ensure that there is a clear process and track of all the critical stuff - meaning **you can't**

be unpleasantly surprised. And if by any chance you are, you have a backup plan in place. You don't need to constantly wonder and panic over and obsess about what just happened, what's happening, and what could happen. You'll know.

- We love to consume media, whether social, news, entertainment, feeds, subscriptions, or chats. But, these have a tendency to **get out of hand**... especially when driven by intelligent algorithms seeking to maximize short-term attention engagement, over long-term mental health. It's ok to cut back - drop out of some groups, set a timer for some apps, recognize when you're caught in a time sink with no real benefits.

- **Don't be envious.** You have a plan for your life that nobody else does - looking at what everyone else is doing can be ok as long as you're learning something, but don't take on the goal that the best part of everyone's life should also be yours. Everyone's got their ups and downs, but they only show off the ups, in their social posts, career updates, and parties.

  No life is up and up, even if you win the lottery, sell your ancestral land, and liquidate the company your grandfather built. You'll be surprised at how quickly that money runs out.

- It's ok to be obsessive, as long as you can channel it into learning. Sure, if you want - spend every minute of your spare time researching stocks, or the best SUV on the market, or your dream holiday. But keep notes as you obsess, and a week later, **take a pause.** See if you're learning anything, if you can come up with a plan on how to put all this activity into action. If not, recognize that you're just wasting time, and maybe move on to something better.

Talk to people in real life.

Sometimes, do nothing. Every minute doesn't have to be full of doing stuff.

It's going to be hard, slow, frustrating, and painful, but anything that feels this bad, usually leads to good things.

• • •

To Do
Physical -

- Create a health file for yourself (physical, IRL)
- Plan for, book, and do a full physical checkup, at least every alternate year.
- Save the checkup reports in this file. Yes, print hard copies.
- Keep a soft copy backup in your preferred online storage.
- Add any and all prescriptions, tests, and reports
- Replicate this for all other family members.

Digital -

- Install an app tracker on your phone that can record and show how much time per app is spent.
- Limit high-time, low-benefit apps to an X amount.
- Set a DND time window if possible. (*If you don't know what I'm talking about, google it. You'll get latest recommendations and links.*)

If you *have* to track a physical activity, track **sleep.** Most fitness trackers and smartwatches can do this, even the basic under-2K ones. Set a target an average minimum of 6 hours. Everyone needs different amounts, but they always need more than they're currently getting.

And if you have absolutely no other physical activity, at least **walk.** But try to have some other physical activity.

Consciously spend some time talking with family and older friends, not just colleagues and partners. It's all too easy for this to get deprioritized.

Minimum 1 holiday per year, at least 3 days, ideally 1 week. Doesn't matter where. This also includes chilling at home with the phone off, watching movies or playing games. You do *not* have to travel to have a holiday. **Mind blown.**

But you *do* need to switch off the damn phone.

• • •

CHAPTER LI

Donations

This is the *last* thing I'll tell you about what to do with your money, I promise.

Don't forget to **give a little** to your favorite charities, once you've done all of the things we have discussed till now.

Not for tax benefits (i.e. evasion), bragging rights, chief guest chair in NGO events, or socialite status.

Do it, because it's the *right thing to do.*

You had your shot, got your opportunity, and made your money, because *you* were lucky enough to be in a situation where you had education, support, a family, friends, a healthy body and working mind, exposure to a professional peer network, a stable government, and no earthquakes, fires, floods, wars, disease, accidents, or other disasters.

A *lot* of people could have been where you are today, probably doing better, if they hadn't happened to have - for no fault of their own - missed out on even *one* of the above. You're not somehow better than them. You only grew up with a better set of circumstances.

You just lucked into a better life.

Imagine yourself in their shoes, or what your life would've looked like, if there had been even one such thing that didn't work out well. An accident, a sickness, an untimely death of a critical person.

Imagine *what a difference* some outside help could've made at that point, for you.

Be that outside help now.

It's good karma.

And while we wrap up this book about money, a final thought.

Never forget, you can't take it with you.

• • •

CHAPTER LII

Your Plan

You've read all the way till here; you learned something. You're ready to change. Now, a plan.

List your goals - what are you going to do, what problems are you going to solve. Take the top 3.

For each one, write -

- **What are you going to do?**
  Keep this as simple as possible. It could be controlling spends, building reserves, saving, anything you feel is most important.
- **What's the result this will have?**
  What is the end result, the exact *figure* that will decide if you succeeded or failed? An X amount is saving, or debt, or reserves, or income?
- **How will you do it?**
  What method will you use? An RD for savings or reserves, an investment instrument, a budget tracker and calendar? Where are you putting it? Stick to what methods you know, or learn it first. Keeps it feasible.
- **What is the problem this will solve?**
  You need to be clear about this. If you're saving, what are you saving for? If you blow your emergency fund on a holiday, you're back at square one. Why are you doing this?
- **When will you finish?**
  Calculate, and set a realistic goal. Maybe not in 3 months, but no point taking 5 years. Review this each month - are you on track? If you don't do it in this much time, you didn't account for something. Try again with a more realistic plan, and factor in what messed up last time.

Copy this template for the next set of goals as well, to be done once you achieve these.

• • •

CHAPTER LIII

Report Card

This is to be used in several places.

1. At the start, when you begin your work.
2. At the end, when you complete your first set of goals.
3. Every time you complete each next set of goals.

This'll show your progress through taking control of money, one step at a time.

My monthly income is _________________.

#	Item	Current	Goal	Score
1	Life Insurance coverage		(12X monthly income)	
2	Health Insurance coverage		(3X monthly income)	
3	Emergency Fund level		(3X monthly income)	
4	Monthly budget		(Started / maintained?)	
5	% Wants and Needs in monthly budget		(< 80% of monthly income)	
6	% Savings or Investments in monthly budget		(> 20% monthly income)	
7	Credit card debt amount		(< 30% monthly income)	
8	Total EMIs and other debts		(< 50% monthly income)	
9	Tax Savers		(100% of limits covered)	
10	Retirement Savings		(Started Y/N?)	

Personal Finance - A Report Card Template

• • •

CHAPTER LIV

Worksheet

Surprise!

As an added bonus, I've made a handy little worksheet for you.

I know Excel can be daunting sometimes, especially if you're starting from scratch. I've set up a basic starter version that'll do some of the first basic tasks.

In this sheet, **you'll be able to -**

- Input some basic information to personalize it as per your situation
- Work out how to get to basic levels of Emergency funds and Insurance coverage
- Understand viability of home or other large purchases and get a recommendation
- Set a monthly budget, structure and set limits on spending, and analyse savings
- Calculate income tax optimization
- Understand inflation and compounding, and how they play off against each other
- Calculate EMIs for goals, along with recommendations
- Get a snapshot of your net worth and diversification risks
- Even visualize a retirement goal and how to get there
- ...and others that I'll keep adding, from time to time.

Subscribe if you want to get those updates, or give a dummy email if you don't want to share the real one; I'm not going to spam, but I will send alerts if any major new functionality's added.

The sheet's a view-only Google sheet, so **make a copy for yourself**, and play around. The more you experiment, the better the insights you get.

There are no scripts, macros, or anything else that will share or leak your data.

https://bit.ly/bwmsheet or https://badwithmoney.blog/worksheet/

Scan for the Bad With Money Worksheet

End

The trouble is... you think you have time.

-The Buddha

Epilogue

So, **that's it.** Hope you find this useful.

I know this - personal finance - is a *complex* area, and subject to a lot of misinformation, misconceptions, and fraudulent activity. There are enough things to be afraid of, here.

It's also very *emotionally* charged, and *hard* to think about calmly and rationally. There'll be emotional triggers, broken dreams, unfair accusations and false promises, deep-seated psychological hang-ups, and many other such similar things. They'll make it hard to plan, or act rationally.

We aren't machines. Money is emotionally important, because of all the emotional things it represents - security, achievement, status, self-esteem.

Hopes and dreams.

This also makes thinking calmly and rationally about money difficult, especially if you're just starting out.

Reading this book... it will *not* make those problems go away. As long as we're human, and we use a medium of exchange, for anything, we'll have these issues.

But I hope by laying out the ideas, approach, and perspectives so far, I've given you some *structure* and *process* by which to organize your own personal finance journey, your goals, aspirations, and constraints.

This book is *not* a comprehensive guide. I've *barely* scratched the surface of most topics covered. The idea's been to give a starting point, a sense of the overall system, that'll allow you to expand and build your own knowledge, create a process that's less frightening, more manageable.

Personal Finance, it's a big subject. It can't be fixed quickly or easily - it's going to take time and effort. A *lot*. But it can be approached with curiosity and adventure, not fear and self-doubt.

Don't FOMO. Everyone's got their own pace of life; some people get to some places, milestones, before others. It'll feel unfair, like you've been cheated out of something, like someone cut the line in Life to get ahead. It'll feel slow. You'll have doubts.

It's *fine*. There are always be tradeoffs made, under the surface of what's publicly visible, that might not work for you.

Set your own pace, set your own goals, plan for them, and stay in control of your life.

• • •

Have a plan.
>Always do your own research.
>Trust, but also verify.
>Make mistakes, but learn from them.
>Have goals, but also an exit strategy.
>Don't panic.

If you can do that, there's nothing to be scared of. It'll all work out.

• • •

Group Think

Early on, I had suggested something along the lines of advice I wish I could have received in the beginning, from someone who had been there and knew the treacherous road that lay ahead.

Second, I also didn't want mine to be the only voice handing out advice - I went out and asked this exact question to people who've been there and done that and drank the Kool-aid.

What do you wish you'd known back then? What do you regret? What did you learn and succeed in? What wisdom or advice do you want to pass on?

The next few pages is a collection of exactly that - where other people add their perspectives on personal finance. I will not filter or edit anything out; here's their advice, as given. As you read it, you'll also see how there isn't one solution or one set of priorities that apply for everyone.

Just like that, you're unique in your goals, situations, and problems. You'll have to build your own custom solution that fits you.

• • •

R is a professional in the financial services industry, with 22 years of experience (including 15+ years managing equity broking, retail and institutional, as well as managing private banking product proposition across asset classes internationally.

Can you list 2-3 suggestions on how you think people should manage personal finance?

Managing personal finance:

Keep it simple, and avoid complicated products.

Focus on basics - Earning - investment = expense - and not the other way round.

Get into the habit of regular saving, then focus on protection (life- term plan, health- medical insurance etc.) and then growth (invest in liquid assets).

Every individual is different, and so is their risk profile. Don't try to copy others for 100% equity or 90% debt exposure. Choose an asset allocation that lets you sleep at night, or avoids you taking rash decisions at the time of market volatility (which is bound to happen.)

Read books written by experienced people on personal finance such as Monika Halan. It will help young people to avoid making simple mistakes and accelerate learning.

Share an example of a choice you made that resulted in a) a good outcome, and b) a mistake that had a negative result?

Good Outcome: Even though I get access to regular tips, ideas and people claiming to make superlative returns from trading, I have not tried to trade aggressively in equity markets similar to social media experts, and that has resulted in avoiding any large blow ups or impact to net worth.

A Mistake: Buying an endowment insurance product without understanding it fully resulted in sub-par returns. Learning: invest only what you understand, and don't go by promises. Always do research before investing.

Any advice you wish someone had given you when you were starting out in early years on how to manage money?

Advice in early years: Read the books written by people who have been successful in equity markets.

. . .

H has over 20 years of experience working across several companies... *"if that adds credibility."*

How would you suggest people approach personal finance?

I think once people start earning reasonably well, they should start saving for the future. In terms of priority, A lot of youngsters these days may have salaries that are insufficient for a reasonably good quality of life; nevertheless there are some thumb rules - try and reduce your rent liability as much as possible in the early years by either sharing with friends, or if you are lucky, staying with parents; learning how to cook and clean (vs ordering all food on app - you will be surprised how much that saves!), and controlling your lifestyle expenditure. Not to say one has to live a Spartan life, but try to ensure your expenses do not get out of hand.

When young, you may have some targets, like further education or settling down or the occasional holiday. Try and work backwards from a budget, use recurring deposits if you have a problem with discipline. Also get a term life insurance once you start earning.

Eventually, your life will get comfortable; you will have consumable money. It is at this time that you have to ensure that you are well-educated on various investments and savings strategies. The early period is quite important especially if you are single or do not yet have children. It is at this time that you will be able to max your investments.

Also this would be a good time to keep a recurring fund aside for your own pension, and any contingencies for your future family as well as your parents in their old age (we're Indian, we take care of the elderly!) Do some research on this, ideally on your own. There are enough youtube videos out there that teach you HOW to handle your money, and keep away from content that tells you WHAT to do. Always remember that financial advisors are there to earn their money, not earn YOU money. They may give good advice and I am sure many are well-meaning people, but it is eventually your money. So seek out advice that tells you HOW.

Any regrets in your personal finance journey?

I personally started out too late since I did not have a high salary to begin with. My first few years in Mumbai were difficult. I also bought a flat early on when I was still single, but the EMI was killing. It would take me a decade to be able to breathe easy with money as a result of good luck and some job changes. One thing I would advise myself was to be a little shameless with money: my then employer went through an IPO and I did not have enough money to take advantage of it. On hindsight I should have borrowed money for that; I was not keen on taking a loan or borrowing from family. As it turned out, a lot of my colleagues made a killing on that IPO (this is my negative story. I should have done the math and listened to wizened share market sharks who were wondering why I would not take a loan)

I would also advise youngsters to try and move out of the country. Unless you are from a very good B-School and in a highly remunerative profession, the saving and investment potential in India is very poor. A few years - not many, less than ten - of earning in USD, AED or SGD would hold you in good stead. INR is overvalued and it is only a matter of time till it crashes.

What worked out well for you?

Though I am comfortable now in my finances - not because I earn tonnes of money - far from it, but because I have had good luck in that my parents/in-laws don't require much support and my own ambitions are fairly modest - I really don't have any strategy or step that turned out to be fortuitous. I have kept a good portion of my earnings in near-liquid for any eventuality, and the rest in equity, pension funds, and mutual funds. I don't speculate or trade. All my investments are geared to finance my children's education and our post-retirement needs.

Hope this little story helps :)

• • •

Parijat Sarkar is a ex-Marketer who switched from a successful corporate profile to a full-time career as stand-up comic, writer, faculty, and Emcee.

What did switching from a corporate salaried job to a freelance consulting / gig profile do to your personal finances?

Surprisingly, I found myself having more savings. I think once you're out of the corporate life with a guaranteed salary, it makes you value both your money, and your time more. You realize and cut a lot of unnecessary expenses; there's less phaltu kharcha like in commuting, 'compulsory' office parties, etc; there's a better and more focused use of time.

For example - if you commute, with the stress and tiredness of the day, or the need to appear presentable, it forces you to take expensive options like cabs because you cannot think of anything else in that state. Similar things apply to where you live, what you prioritize, etc.

Once I was out of that rut, I could focus and think clearly and work on what was actually critical.

The result? Never in my wildest dreams did I imagine that a home loan could be paid off within 6 years instead of 25, and that too after quitting!

Having a regular salary stops you thinking, makes you lazy. You always assume the money will be there next month, so you make poorer decisions.

You also think very hard before taking on loans. When I wanted to buy a car, I took the loan from my mom and paid her back through an RD route. It saves me time in the process, I get a better deal, I'm not paying exorbitant fees to loan companies, and there's less paperwork, transfers, hypothecation, etc.

And at the end you get a car, not the headache of a car loan.

Any other general advice?

ULIP *zeher* hai. It should not exist as a product. Take term only insurance, or don't take anything at all. I made that mistake long back and I finally reached a point where I had to terminate prematurely. You have to think then of whether to invest more money in hopes of getting even some back, or take your losses and move on.

Also, don't take financial advice or buy financial products from family members.

• • •

S, Fractional CMO - Data-Driven Growth Architect

Term Insurance for family.

Health Insurance to protect.

Index funds with the lowest overheads for investments and Credit cards for emergency liquidity.

Of course: I have already finished slaving for my house :)

• • •

Manu Prasad has been investing since 2004; former CMO of Scripbox, on track to be financially independent by the end of 2025. ?

Can you list 2-3 suggestions on how you think people should manage personal finance? What's some of the most important things to consider?

Why: From the time I got serious about personal finance (mid-late thirties) I have thought about it in the frame of Life Plan -> Financial Plan -> Career Plan. Understanding what you need, and want, in life gives you an idea of how much to aim for. That requires some deep thought. But that intentionality will help you make conscious choices that you will most likely not regret.

What: Choose the right investments. I am a big believer in equity, and have been investing in mutual funds for a couple of decades, two years after I started working. Its risk-reward rate is great, and it has liquidity. Don't worry too much about specific funds, timing the market and so on. Stay away from 'get rich soon' schemes because it's mostly the people who run it that get rich, not you.

How: More clarity will happen in your thirties (relatively), but that doesn't mean you wait till then to get going. Start with your first salary. The biggest game changer in investing is compounding. Investing lots of money later in life won't make up for lost time. Instead, up your investing by 10-20% each year, and let the magic of compounding work for you. Focus on playing the long game and staying disciplined. Invest first, and then spend, that also keeps lifestyle bloat away. As your wealth increases, diversify it. In the words of James Clear, "Always be prepared to absorb a big hit. Always be focused enough to create a big win. Diversified enough to survive, concentrated enough to matter."

An example of a choice made that resulted in a good outcome, and a mistake that had a negative result?

Good outcome: Starting early in equity and avoiding common advice like FDs, LIC etc, though I have to admit that at that time, it was more a bet than a certainty.

Bad outcome: Purchasing property because a friend recommended it. Be careful about whom you take investment advice from.

Any advice you wish someone had given you when you were starting out in early years on how to manage money?

Wealth is health. Mental health. Money is a shock absorber that can, if used correctly, help you cope with a lot of things. Our education does not give us a structured understanding on how to build wealth.I was lucky enough to have someone get me started on equity early. Today, options are exploding, and everyone is in a hurry to get rich quickly. 10 minute delivery isn't the answer to everything. 'Get rich slowly' is probably a healthier path.

• • •

Chintan Banker has worked in the Financial Services Industry (in India & Australia) for over 20 years. Most of his experience has been in Strategic Financial Advice and Wealth Management.

Can you list 2-3 suggestions on how you think people should manage personal finance? What's some of the most important things to consider?

Here are a few suggestions that might be useful for people just starting out in their careers:

• Budgeting: Lot of people Save what is left at the end of the month/ week. My clients have always benefited from a change of approach – Save first and then spend what is left to spend. Prioritize savings—aim for at least 10%-20% of your income if possible.

• Build an Emergency Fund: Life is unpredictable, so having 3-6 months' worth of expenses saved can help you make sure your long term plans are not derailed. Nothing worse than having to fire sale assets.

• Power of compounding: Start small Start early. SIPs (in India) are a great way. As they say, time in the market, not timing the market.

An example of a choice made that resulted in a good outcome, and a mistake that had a negative result?

Personal Experiences:

• Good Outcome: Starting an SIP (Systematic Investment Plan) early in my career was one of the best decisions I made. Its more the discipline.

• Mistake: Like most Gujaratis who think stock trading is in their blood... initially in my career, I have (more than once) made the mistake of putting a lot of my savings into a single stock that was "hot" at the time. Guess, I had to learn the hard way about the importance of diversification.

Any advice you wish someone had given you when you were starting out in early years on how to manage money?

Advice I Wish I Knew Early On:

• Lot of people serious about building wealth, focus all energy on saving more... which is great, but its not enjoyable when you cannot Live Life.

• Have learnt, it is a lot easier to try and earn more (which can help save more) than just save a lot from what you currently earn.

• • •

Davinia D'Souza heads the Pan-India Banking Channel at BOI AXA Investments Managers Private Limited

Can you list 2-3 suggestions on how you think people should manage personal finance? What's some of the most important things to consider?

(A) Think Long Term when it comes to investments. Today's generation and culture revolves around "quick and easy money". But remember "Rome was not built in a day". Sustained wealth creation is a process, as is building a corpus

(B) Be disciplined when it comes to investments and try not to be influenced by the "noise" around you. Remember "Slow and steady wins the race"

(C) Patience not Panic is key when markets are volatile. If your investments are fundamentally good, they will revive and deliver as per expectations

(D) Diversification is the key. Never put all your eggs in one basket no matter how attractive the return or payout. Also, avoid the risk of Overdiversification!

An example of a choice made that resulted in a good outcome, and a mistake that had a negative result?

(A) Started SIPs and lumpsum investments in Mutual Funds (diversified as per risk appetite and time horizon) over 20 years back. Had professional fund managers backed by research teams handling the portfolios so didn't have to worry about short term changes and exits. Over the last 20 years, all the fund managers have beaten inflation and have given at least a 12% plus annualized return (equity) thus leading to a good compounding benefit.

(B) Invested in a couple of stocks directly based on hearsay and burnt my fingers badly! Hence, don't let the "noise in the market" disturb your long term wealth creation strategy!

Any advice you wish someone had given you when you were starting out in early years on how to manage money?

Don't invest from what is left after spending, instead spend what is left after investing. This simple mantra can help build your retirement kitty even if you start late in life.

• • •

G has 30 years' experience in Marketing, Insurance, Consulting, Fintech & Business Transformation

Can you list 2-3 suggestions on how you think people should manage personal finance? What's some of the most important things to consider?

The 3 suggestions I would make are :

1) Time in the market is more than timing the market

2) Diversify your investments to ensure you are protecting yourself from "correlation risk". But do not over-diversify..It almost never pays off

3) If investing in stocks, look at the company's free cash flow..most likely you won't go wrong..

An example each of a choice you made that resulted in -

a) a good outcome?

I primarily invest in US markets (since my cost of living in Dubai is USD pegged). I invested in a stock that holds a near monopoly in a very specific niche. The price nearly quadrupled in 4 years. (No it was not Nvidia). Not a bad dollar return.

b) A mistake that had a negative result?

I got into speculative investing in gold futures early on in my life influenced by some friends.. although I did not fully understand the dynamics fully. I paid the price for it.

• • •

Nolan Michael Mascarenhas is a Financial Wealth Advisor holding a diverse range of client portfolios under his franchise of Nuvama Wealth Management Advisory Services Limited. He helps aspiring and seasoned investors plan in order to be Financially free to maximise their true potential in Life and not Financially independent.

Can you list 2-3 suggestions on how you think people should manage personal finance? What's some of the most important things to consider?

For someone starting out with personal finance, I would like to focus on these non-negotiable essential rules:

1. Spend Less Than You Earn

This is the foundation of financial health. If your spending exceeds your income, you'll rely on debt, which can spiral out of control.

Track your income and expenses diligently (I like to use a free simple app called Monefy for daily expenses)

Prioritize needs over wants and stick to a budget.

Avoid lifestyle inflation as your income grows.

2. Pay Yourself First

Why: Building savings early ensures you're prepared for emergencies, opportunities, and long-term goals.

Set aside a fixed percentage of your income (early starters go aggressive to ease up as you become older) for savings or investments before paying bills or spending.

Build an emergency fund of 3–6 months of your salary/monthly income worth of expenses.

Automate savings to make it a habit and minimize temptation.

3. Avoid High-Interest Debt

Debt like credit card balances or payday loans can cripple your financial growth due to compounding interest.

Only borrow what you can repay comfortably (e.g., for assets like a home or education).

Pay off high-interest debt aggressively, starting with credit cards if you have any.

These three principles—spending wisely, saving consistently, and avoiding bad debt—are the cornerstones.

An example each of a choice you made that resulted in -

a) a good outcome?

Good practices would be to start investing early on in the markets and SIP my way across a diverse risk averse portfolio and forgetting to withdraw any of it for 15 years even when temptations prevailed.

b) A mistake that had a negative result?

A bad example would be me not being able to close a credit card outstanding on 200 rupees that affected by CIBIL score 19 years later till date.

Any advice you wish someone had given you when you were starting out in early years on how to manage money?

The lure of temptation and the propensity to spend for the moment is how the system is designed to derail one of the path and course that ideally needs to be followed. Think rich, live within your means and must haves vs wants is the golden key that differentiates one from having to work till retirement.

Smart savings in diversified portfolios - real estate, commercial ventures are always on the rise over the inflation matrix of today. Study interest rates before putting your money down to financial institutions and you will always be ahead of the curve. I personally stay away from depreciating assets such as vehicles, fancy 1 lac smart phones etc which solve a purpose momentarily but are a honey trap once attained for something more luxurious and the want is never ending vs the need for consumption.

• • •

Glossary

80CC, 80D, etc

Tax-exemption categories under which you can show investments made to get a tax writeoff. Specific investments are eligible and each category comes with a cap.

Aadhar

Identity + biometrics document issued to all Indian citizens, to be used as proof of identity, age, and address.

AI

Artificial Intelligence. Used in reference to ChatGPT, Perplexity, CoPilot, Grok, or others

APR

Annual percentage rate: the interest charged on loans and credit cards. Applied to total outstanding (not just unpaid)

Assets

Things you own that gain value over time, like investments, gold, property, etc.

ATM

Automated Teller Machine - where you go to take out physical cash when your phone is dead and credit card is declined

AUM

Assets Under Management - how much money is a mutual fund managing? More is usually better.

BFSI

Banking, Financial Services, and Insurance - a category of all finance-oriented companies

BHK

Bedroom-Hall-Kitchen - used to designated the typology / size of a house, eg. a 2-bed is 2BHK

Blue chip

A way to designate very good quality organizations in terms of stability, size, resources, risk-aversiveness, and future prospects. Not necessarily a guarantee of best returns.

Budget

A plan for designating / allocating resources towards planned expenses and investments in a given time period. Can be from level of individual to nation.

CA

Chartered Accountant - the guy who helps you file taxes and suggests investments

CASA

Current Account Savings Account - the standard 2-account setup at a bank

Cash Flow

The movement of money - how much comes in, and what it gets spent on, on a recurring basis

Cashless

Applied to medical insurance at hospitals. Cashless options mean you don't need to pay and claim for covered medical expenses, they are billed directly by the hospital to the insurer.

CC

Credit Card

Challan

Proof of / Demand for payment made to a government entity

CIBIL

Credit Information Bureau India Limited. The guys who track your loans, repayment history, spending patterns, and give a score that is used by banks to decide if you get a loan or not, and the interest rate thereof.

CMO

Chief Marketing Officer - one of the senior positions in upper management levels, usually reporting to Managing Director / Owner, and responsible for the marketing function.

Compounding

The process in which money saved earns interest, which in turn itself earns interest, leading to exponential growth in the long term

Coverage

Insurance context - what specific conditions / diseases are eligible to be compensated for. Can also refer to the total amount of money available for the same.

Credentials

A. Security key / password / rights to access something

B. History and repudiation of a person or organization

Crypto

Cryptocurrency, usually used to refer a speculative digital asset class

CTC

Cost-to-company - the total amount an organization s prepared to spend on you, including salary, perks, and incentives. This is what usually gets written in offer letters.

Debt

Money that you owe to someone, i.e. what you need to pay

Diversification

The practice of having a variety of different investments in different sizes, instruments, and categories in order to spread risk and increase stability

Dividends

Periodic payments received from companies whose shares you own, as a part of their profits. Used for building passive income streams

Diwali

Festival in India, marking the start of the festive season, and accompanied by increased consumption, advertising, and spending. Usually implies high levels of offers and discounts as well as new product launches

DND

Do Not Disturb - a phone setting that silences calls, messages and notifications

Dropbox

An online file storage service

DYOR

Do Your Own Research - phrase used to encourage reader not to take recommendations at face value and investigate on his own before taking any decisions

ECS

Electronic Clearing System - setting in bank accounts to enable automated payments and scheduled money transfers

ELSS

Equity Linked Saving Scheme - a type of mutual fund where investments are eligible for tax credit / writeoff, if within limits and eligible categories. Thus gives dual benefit of returns and tax savings

Emergency Fund

Corpus of funds kept in reserve to be used only in case of emergencies, like job loss or natural disasters

EMI

Equated Monthly Installment - the monthly amount you pay to clear a loan, including both the loan amount and interest amount.

EPF

Employees' Provident Fund - a government-supported scheme to offer employees a means to save for retirement. Offers a decent interest rate and tax benefits, but applies certain limits and conditions on withdrawal

ESOP

Employee Stock Ownership Plan - a benefit offered by private organizations granting a certain volume of shares, or option to purchase shares at preferential rates

ETF

Exchange Traded Fund - a basket of stocks traded on stock exchanges. Offers diversification without high investment requirements.

Excel

Microsoft Excel, alternately used with Google Sheets in this book. Software used for mathematical calculations, planning, analysis, and projections

Expense

Something you need to give money for. Duh.

F1

Formula One - referring to both the sport of high-end car racing, as well as the types of cars used in it

FD

Fixed Deposit - a low-risk, bank-guaranteed investment earning moderate returns

Fee

Charge applied to services rendered, usually as a % of the amount invested

Finfluencer

Social media personality specializing in finance-related themes

FIRE

Financially Independent, Retire Early - the goal of building sufficient retirement wealth and passive income so that traditional paid employment becomes optional

Flexi cap

A category of mutual funds and similar investment instruments that cover a range of companies of different market sizes, where the proportion varies as per changes in market conditions

FOMO

Fear of missing out - a form of greed where a person fears losing a perceived opportunity. Usually linked to hype / rumour.

Fraandship

A social engineering technique employed by scammers offering projected romantic / sexual relationships or benefits, often online, in order to extract sensitive information, money, or blackmail material. Usually targets horny, lonely or socially awkward people.

Fund manager

Manager of a mutual fund or investment instrument, in charge of actively buying / selling assets contained within the fund.

GST

Goods and Services Tax - indirect tax applied by the government. Increases prices, and is usually independent from any other taxes you might already be paying

GoT

Game of Thrones. Context: a place of ambition, betrayal, conspiracy, deals, envy, fear, greed, and hatred.

Health Insurance

Insurance applied specifically to illness and medical treatment scenarios

Hopium

A form of optimistic self-delusion or wishful thinking, in trying to convince oneself that a positive outcome is likely. Causes people to ignore red flags and make poor financial decisions, ignoring data for feeling.

HR

Human Resources - the team in an organization responsible for managing and communicating about employee compensation, benefits, and salary structure.

I-T

Income Tax. Usually used in reference to the Income Tax department, hyphenated to differentiate from Information Technology (IT)

Identity theft

The technique of illegally obtaining access to someone else's personal data and credentials in order to conduct financial transactions or commitments without their consent or knowledge. Perpetrator takes benefits and leaves the original owner to suffer consequences. It's not a joke.

Ikigai

Japanese philosophy centered around finding fulfilment and wellbeing from meaningful and enjoyable activities related to one's own personality, skills and character, as opposed to doing an activity for only payment.

Impulse buy

The act of purchasing something on the spur of the moment because of emotional triggers, rather than by a rational data-driven decision.

Income

The money you get and have the ability to spend. Usually refers to salary, own business revenue, interest or dividend payouts.

Index funds

A type of fund that tracks performance of companies in a certain index, by replicating the content of that index. Usually passive and cheaper than actively-managed funds.

Inflation

The phenomenon of prices increasing over time as purchasing power degrades. Usually a result of very high economy growth or fiscal mismanagement by a government.

Inheritance

Receiving money that belonged to someone else (usually a relative) legally willed to you in the event of their death.

INR

India Rupee - currency used in India. Used interchangeably with 'Rs.'

Interest

Reward received on a periodic basis for saving. Banks usually give this by using your deposited funds in loans to others and paying you a share of fees earned.

IPO

Initial Public Offering - when a company goes public (gets listed on the stock market) by offering shares for purchase by investors. Used to increase available cash resources for growth. When you participate in an IPO, you get some shares as per a predetermined value, after which value is decided by market dynamics.

IRL

In Real Life - i.e. as opposed to online / digital / social media experiences and interactions

IT

Information Technology, usually used in the context of a company's IT department

ITR

Income Tax Return - the acknowledgement given by the Income Tax department as proof of taxes paid. Used as a means of income validation to

3rd parties and in future audits.

Karoshi

Japanese term for the phenomenon of death caused by overwork, usually characterized by highly stressful work environments, creating inability to self-regulate health requirements leading to increasingly poor health and finally collapse.

KBC

Kaun Banega Crorepati - Indian game show where winners in a general knowledge quiz environment advance through stages to win large (life-changing) sums of money.

KTM

Refers to KTM Duke, a brand of motorcycles appreciated for both good looks and high performance while remaining affordable. Popular in urban environments.

KYC

Know Your Customer - the process by which financial institutions collect personal data of potential customers in order to validate identity and initiate services. Usually involves sharing of sensitive identity documentation.

Largecap

Classification of companies categorized by a large market capitalization, implying deep pockets, large resources, and long-term stability.

Liabilities

Stuff you owe to someone else, debts that need to be paid

LIC

Life Insurance Corporation of India. India's largest insurer, operating via a network of grassroots-level agents to sell life insurance policies and similar products.

Life Insurance

Insurance cover that pays out in the event of death of the policyholder

Liquidity

The amount of money available, or how easy it is to sell / buy an asset. Low liquidity means waiting a while for the right buyer at the right price (eg. with property). High liquidity products can be easily and quickly bought and sold.

Loan

An amount of money borrowed (usually from a bank) and paid back with some interest charged

LTA

Leave Travel Allowance - a sum of money that can be claimed once every 2 years for domestic travel in India

MBA

Masters in Business Administration - a post-graduate course in management usually perceived as a must-have for a corporate management career, usually with expectation of high pay.

MCap

Market Capitalization - the total value of a company's public shares X share price

MF

Mutual Fund - an investment instrument that purchases a group of shares for a defined period of time, usually on a periodic recurring plan.

MFA

Multi-Factor Authentication - a security setting for digital platforms that requires authentication via both a username+password and a separate email, sms, or app based validation before allowing access. Important for platforms where high cash value assets or personal data is stored.

Midcap

Companies with a market capitalization in the mid range; perceived as higher-risk, higher return than large caps, but having a measure of credibility / reputation.

MLM

Multi-Level Marketing - usually associated with beauty products or household goods, run by housewives in the 50s. Now expanded to cover a vast range of products.

Also usually end up being pyramid schemes or otherwise exploitative, trapping people into an unsustainable system while making the owner rich.

Money

Something commonly accepted as a medium to purchase goods or services, with a fixed quantity set for each product (price)

Multi cap

Investment fund containing companies of different capitalization sizes, usually in a fixed proportion.

NBFC

Non-Banking Financial Company - companies dealing in financial products and services, but not proper banks. Usually deal in loans, investment platforms, insurance, wealth management, etc. Less regulated than banks.

NFC

Near-Field Communications - a feature of higher-end phones that allows credit card or access card operations to be done by projecting a short-range field to the recipient device. Convenient but dangerous as it opens a potential vulnerability for unauthorized transactions.

NGO

Non-Government Organization - charities, groups or organizations working for the public good, supported by donations.

NPS

National Pension Scheme - a financial tool offered / supported by the government for investing in a fund for retirement planning. Offers some tax benefits and moderate returns.

NRI

Non-Resident Indian - a person of Indian origin (holding an Indian nationality and passport) residing outside India. Usually free from paying taxes in India.

NSC

National Savings Certificate - a financial tool offered / supported by the government for investing in a fund for retirement planning. Offers some tax benefits and moderate returns. Available via post office outlets.

Offshore

A type of fund focusing on investing in companies based outside India. Offers a convenient diversification option to hedge risks outside India's economy and increase global investing exposure, without incurring high fees and complexity of directly purchasing foreign equity.

PAN

Permanent Account Number - a government-issued identification used as the primary identity in all tax-related activities, including income.

Personal Finance

A set of activities associated with managing the flow of income, expenses, and investments relevant for an individual (unlike corporate finance)

PII

Personally Identifiable Information - sensitive data that specifically identifies an individual, eg. phone, email, address, credit card number, Aadhar, etc. Dangerous if leaked and misused.

Pivot table

A function inside of Excel / Google Sheets to process and tabulate moderate amounts of raw data and aid in analysis and information processing.

Portfolio

A group of related assets - eg. equities, mutual funds, etc. Can also be used in a broader context, eg. Investment portfolio referring to multiple types.

POS

Point of Sale - the machines in shops where you swipe your card to make a payment

PPF

Personal Provident Fund - a financial tool offered / supported by the government for investing in a fund for retirement planning. Offers some tax benefits and moderate returns. Available via national banks.

PR

Public Relations - a team within a company responsible for managing relevant stories and information in public media like news, reports, and social media.

PRAN

Permanent Retirement Account Number - the identifier used in NPS accounts

Premium

The periodic amount paid to an insurance company to maintain insurance coverage

Premium receipt

Acknowledgement received from an insurance company that premium has been paid

PS5

Playstation 5 - high-end gaming console, a luxury product

QR (Code)

A grid pattern readable by mobile phones, containing encoded information about a link, some data, or payments.

QSR

Quick Service Restaurant, also used for quick-commerce apps. Instamart, Blinkit, Zepto, etc. Can encourage impulsive shopping at whim, rather than planned groceries and meals.

RD

Recurring Deposit - an amount you can voluntarily choose to set up in a bank where a periodic amount of money is deducted from your savings account and added to a deposit account. Requires a committed period of payments. Earns low to moderate returns, but primarily used as a method of enforced saving.

REIT

Real Estate Investment Trust - an investment instrument similar to mutual funds where you purchase a share of commercial property, and receive dividends from collected rent. Used to increase exposure to real estate investing without the need for blocking large amounts of money and the headache of property purchase and management.

Rider (insurance)

Add-on coverage to include special conditions in insurance policies (eg. specific diseases, or disabilities) not offered in the standard package. Increases premium amount but makes the policy a better protector.

Risk

The chance of something bad happening. Used as a measure of how likely to fail something is, and the potential impact of that failure.

Saving

Money you don't spend, repay, or lose.

Scam

When someone fools you into parting with your money, data, or property under false promises or pretenses.

Sector

The area of industry a company belongs to, defined by the type of business model or product it deals with. Sectors usually follow their own unique macro cycle and affect all companies in that sector together.

SEO

Search Engine Optimization - a technique in digital marketing technology used to increase the likelihood of a preferred piece of content appearing more in results for online searches.

SGB

Sovereign Gold Bond - a financial tool offered / supported by the government for investing specifically in gold. Offers some tax benefits, returns linked to performance of gold as an asset. Available at banks at periodic intervals.

SIM Card

Subscriber Identity Module - the chip you put in your phone that gives you a phone number. Obtained from mobile operators via stores / online after KYC. if lost or cloned, may allow a scammer access to your accounts and identities

SIP

Systematic Investment Plan - a technique of investing where a fixed amount is deducted and invested in a preselected instrument on a set date each month / quarter. Used to ensure regular investing in a simplified process.

Smallcap

Companies with low market capitalization; perceived as highest-risk, but with the greatest room to grow. Have little or no credibility / reputation, and may easily fail.

SME

Small or Medium Enterprise - smaller companies, usually less organized and local.

Stock Market

A place where shares and similar instruments can be bought and sold. Usually online.

Stocks

A part-ownership in a publicly listed company, entitling you to a share of profit and benefit from appreciation inshare value.

Subscription

Some product service you pay for on a regular basis

SUV

Sport Utility Vehicle - a medium to large sized car, usually perceived as more premium, or conferring higher status

SWP

Systematic Withdrawal Plan - a cashing-out technique where you automatically sell a part of an invested fund and receive cash on a regular fixed period. Used as a way to create an even, secondary income stream.

Tax

Money you pay the government for maintaining and building infrastructure, national security, and public works and services.

Tax Slab

The amount you pay in tax. The very poor pay nothing; the more you earn, the more you pay, in increasing slabs.

Term

The period of coverage in an insurance policy, or duration of any financial instrument like a MF.

UAN

Universal Account Number - the identifier used in employee provident funds

ULIP

Unit Linked Insurance Plan - a hybrid investment instrument offering exposure to equities (like a mutual fund) but also with insurance coverage. Offers moderate returns and some tax benefits.

UPI

Unified Payments Interface - a system to enable digital payments via mobile phones in a fast, easy and seamless way. Money is transferred directly from sender account to receiver account via a transfer initiated on a UPI app via number, account, or QR code.

USB

Universal Serial Bus - a port for data access and transfer in your computer / phone. In this context, it refers to a USB storage drive - a small storage device that plugs into your computer and can be used to store data.

Value

What something is worth, or what you are ready to pay for it. Not necessarily it's price, and not always in currency.

Wealth

Something you have that gives freedom, time, and security, and can be used to generate income or invested. Not necessarily the same as money.

Wealth Manager

A specialist financial expert - individual or organization - who focuses on managing the investment growth, tax protection, de-risking, and operations of money and cash flow for wealthy clients.

Whatsapp University

The continuous barrage of rumor, hype, misinformation, and FOMO that travels across user groups on the Whatsapp platform (and sometimes in other online forums, platforms, and comment sections) leading to poor decision-making.

YT

Youtube.

Acknowledgements

There's a *lot* of stuff that's contributed towards making this book happen, over a long time. Some from general news, books, podcasts, movies and articles; some very specific, hard-worked contributions from friends and colleagues.

Thanks to Nolan Mascarenhas, Davinia D'Souza, Chintan Banker, Manu Prasad, Parijat Sarkar, and many, *many* others for their insights and contributions.

Other references, ideas, checklists, inspirations, and learnings have been distilled from the following, at least as far as I can remember. There may - in fact, definitely *are* - *many* more I might have absorbed over the years, subconsciously chewed on them, and then brought them up again in some form or the other while writing. If you recognize any, please accept them as a tribute - and let me know, I'll be happy to add to the list in subsequent editions.

- Movies & Shows - definitely worth an entertaining watch even from a non-finance perspective, but also *highly* educational.

  - *Dumb Money*, 2023
  - *Eat The Rich*, 2022
  - *Scam 1992*, 2020
  - *The Big Short*, 2015
  - *Inside Job*, 2008
  - *Boiler Room*, 2000
  - *Wall Street*, 1987

- Podcasts worth following

  - *Death, Sex, and Money*, with Anna Sale
  - *Dev Raga Personal Finance*
  - *Money Guy Show*, with Brian Preston & Bo Hanson
  - *Money Talks - The Economist*
  - *Money Stuff*, with Matt Levine
  - *Morningstar Investing Insights*
  - *Paisa Vaisa*, with Anupam Gupta

- *Planet Money by NPR*
  - *Rule Breaker Investing,* with David Gardner
  - *Slate Money,* with Felix Salmon

- Books worth reading and re-reading

  - *Atomic Habits* - James Clear
  - *Money Works* - Abhijeet Kolapkar
  - *Rich Dad, Poor Dad* - Robert Kiyosaki
  - *The Alamanack of Naval Ravikant* - Naval Ravikant
  - *The Bitcoin Standard* - Saifedean Ammous
  - *The Intelligent Investor* - Ben Graham
  - *The Psychology of Money* - Morgan Housel
  - *The Richest Man In Babylon* - George Clason

- Quotes attributed to -

  - Albert Einstein
  - Ancient Chinese Proverbs
  - Chuck Palahniuk
  - Gautam Buddha
  - Gaurav Kapoor (*for that one 2024 stand-up joke the fans among you noticed!*)
  - George Carlin
  - Kevin Mitnick
  - Naval Ravikant
  - Robert Kiyosaki
  - Warren Buffet

• • •

9 798889 744518